KOREABOO

BY MICHELLE LIM DAVIDSON

CURRENCY PRESS
The performing arts publisher

**GRIFFIN
THEATRE
COMPANY**

CURRENT THEATRE SERIES

First published in 2025
by Currency Press Pty Ltd,
Gadigal Land, Suite 310, 46–56 Kippax Street, Surry Hills, NSW 2010, Australia
enquiries@currency.com.au
www.currency.com.au

in association with Griffin Theatre Company

Typeset by Brighton Gray for Currency Press.
Cover image shows Michelle Lim Davidson; cover photography by David Boon.
Cover design by Susu Studio.

Currency Press acknowledges the Traditional Owners of the Country on which we live and work. We pay our respects to all Aboriginal and Torres Strait Islander Elders, past and present.

A catalogue record for this book is available from the National Library of Australia

Contents

I acknowledge the Traditional Custodians of the land on which *Koreaboo* has been created and will be performed—the Gadigal people of the Eora Nation—and I extend that respect to all Aboriginal and Torres Strait Islander peoples. I pay my respects to Elders past and present and recognise their deep and enduring connection to this land, to its skies, seas, and waterways—which have always been places of story, gathering, and culture.

This land is special to me because it has shaped my voice as an artist.

I have laughed, wept, danced, and dreamed here. I have learned how to tell stories here—and how to listen. My appreciation for Country has been enriched by the teachings of First Nations friends, artists, and Elders, who continue to show me what it means to belong, to remember, and to care for community.

Always was, always will be—Aboriginal land.

Koreaboo was produced by Griffin Theatre Company and first performed at Downstairs Theatre, Belvoir St Theatre, Gadigal Country, Sydney, on 14 June 2025, with the following cast and creatives:

HANNAH / GAM — Michelle Lim Davidson

UMMA — Heather Jeong

Director, Jessica Arthur
Dramaturg, Julian Lanarch
Designer, Mel Page
Lighting Designer, Kate Baldwin
Composer and Sound Designer, Brendon Boney
Design Associate, James Stibilj
Development Associate, Andrew Undi Lee
Production Manager, Sherydan Simson
Stage Manager, Jen Jackson
Community Engagement Lead, Korean Adoptees in Australia Network (KAIAN)

CHARACTERS

UMMA/SOON HEE. A Korean woman who runs a small convenience mart in Itaewon. Practical, unsentimental, and unexpectedly funny. Hannah's birth mother.

HANNAH. A Korean Australian adoptee. This is only her second time in Korea. Outwardly composed, inwardly uncertain—reaching for a connection that has moved on without her.

GAM. Performed by the actor playing Hannah. Not quite a ghost, not quite Hannah—somewhere in between.

VOICES. Various Korean-speaking roles. Pre-recorded audio used throughout the script to represent background characters, announcements, or offstage dialogue. Heard but not seen.

KOREABOO

Koreaboo is a term used to describe someone, often a non-Korean individual, who is overly enthusiastic about Korean culture. They might exhibit an intense interest in Korean pop culture, music, fashion, language, or other aspects of Korean society that can sometimes border on obsession or become culturally insensitive.

SETTING

Present day. Seoul, South Korea.

A family-run convenience mart tucked away in a quieter side alley of Itaewon—a district known for its nightlife and diversity. Once thriving, the area around the mart has seen reduced foot traffic, edged out by franchises, and shifting trends. The shop has survived by adapting: the owner picked up English from tourists and binge-watches American TV shows during slow hours. Nestled near hotels and a wholesale market, the mart clings to its corner of the neighbourhood with stubborn charm.

Despite the mart's age, it's neat and clean. DIY fixes abound—sticky tape marks from long-lost posters, handwritten labels, shelves added over time rather than replaced. The walls are a creamy egg colour—impossible to tell if that was their original shade or if they've aged into it over time. Garden gnomes are carefully placed throughout. The back wall is dedicated to a stunning display of toilet paper and a towering pyramid of Spam, their pristine packaging a stark contrast to the worn linoleum beneath them. Rows of ramyun and snacks line the shelves, with a microwave and boiling water station nearby. Cans of WD-40 are nestled next to ankle socks and kitchen tools. A sun-bleached cardboard cut-out of an outdated star grins from the corner. Stands of sunglasses, USB cords, and beauty products sway—an odd assortment with no clear connection, yet arranged like an impressive game of Tetris, more practical than intentional.

The cash register sits beside a lucky cat figurine, its mechanical paw still waving, though one eye remains permanently shut, as if winking or caught mid-blink. Bottles of soju and beer rattle gently against cartons of milk. A small display of fresh fruit and vegetables rests beside an old fridge. On the counter, a neat cluster of perfect persimmons catches the glow of the television. It's a patchwork of past and present.

LANGUAGE

This script contains dialogue in both English and Korean, reflecting the cultural and linguistic complexity at the heart of the story. Korean is presented in three parts to support accessibility for readers, performers, and creative teams. Example:

> UMMA: What I say? 이감은 얼마예요? I gam-eun eolmayeyo? (How much is this persimmon?)

The Korean translation in the script is a guide—a starting point. It can and should be personalised to suit the performer playing umma, reflecting her rhythm, tone, and emotional truth.

Korean, like many languages, shifts depending on formality, age, and relationship. Umma's dialogue moves between informal, familiar speech and more restrained or formal registers. These shifts carry emotional weight and may be adapted in rehearsal to reflect the nuances of her character. This flexibility extends to offstage voices as well, whose tone and register may be adjusted to support the dramatic context and the performer's interpretation. The Hangul text included is a placeholder and should be revised in consultation with the performer(s) to ensure linguistic and emotional authenticity.

Romanisation

Revised Romanisation appears in following the Hangul, offering pronunciation support for non-Korean-speaking performers.

Translation

English translations are included in parentheses () providing meaning and context without interrupting the rhythm or intent of the scene.

NOTE ON TEXT

Slashes (/) are used to indicate a sharp interruption or overlap in dialogue—when one character cuts off another or when two characters speak at the same time. Ellipses (…) signal a trailing off, hesitation, or an unfinished thought, often conveying emotional weight, uncertainty, or a pause in rhythm.

FOOTNOTES

Footnotes are used throughout the script to explain specific cultural references, phrases, or items that may be unfamiliar to some readers or audiences. These notes are intended to provide context, not translation, and help preserve the nuance, humour, or emotional weight of the original language and setting.

LYRICS

The K-pop song lyrics included in the script are placeholders and have been invented for dramaturgical purposes. In production, some lyrics, as indicated by the footnotes will be replaced with actual K-pop songs selected by the creative team, subject to rights and permissions. The lyrics for 'Arirang', the traditional Korean folk song, are in the public domain. A specific verse has been chosen to align thematically with the play's narrative and emotional arc.

PERFORMANCE NOTES

Code-switching in *Koreaboo* is character-driven and emotionally charged. Korean is used when it feels natural—whether to communicate, create distance, express humour, or reveal identity. The rhythm of speech may shift across languages. Misunderstandings or mistranslations are intentional, underscoring themes of disconnection and reconnection.

This playtext went to press before the end of rehearsals and may differ from the play as performed.

SCENE ONE

The stage is shrouded in darkness.

*BOOM! The powerful, pulsating beats of a famous K-pop song[1]
explode. Light strobes. Haze unfurls. The line between reality and
fantasy blurs—it's unclear if the music is blasting from a nearby club
or from the mart itself.*

UMMA: 아이고![2] AIGO! (Oh my!)

> *A click. A flicker. Fluorescent lights snap on. The illusion
> vanishes. It's not theatrical haze, it's smoke coming from the
> fridge. The K-pop song is swallowed by the tinny jingle of a
> K-pop reality competition—*Star Power*—playing on the TV.
> Perched atop a stepladder, half inside the fridge, is* UMMA. *Her
> purple-tipped perm puffs through the top of her oversized visor
> like steam. She's mid-task, mid-life—a canary in a cage.*

> HANNAH *stands inside with her suitcase. It's her second trip to Korea,
> but still disorienting. She looks local enough for people to speak to
> her in fluent Korean—until she answers in Australian English. Their
> faces shift, confused. Her blazer, meant to make a good impression,
> now feels like a costume. She's trying, but out of place.*

> UMMA, *by contrast, is effortlessly herself—practical, unfussy. She
> looks like she set out on a hike and ended up running a mart. Floral
> pants. A faux Burberry scarf. A bright orange apron. Her 'ajumma
> crown'—a plastic sun visor on her head indoors, at night. Its purpose
> unclear. No lipstick. No ceremony. No effort wasted on the occasion.*

[*Friendly customer-service voice*] 이거 어떻게 하지? 잠깐만요. 금방
갈게요. *Igeo eotteoke haji? jamkkanmanyo. geumbang galgeyo.*
(How do I do this? Wait a moment. I'll be with you soon.)

---

1. The song used in this scene should reflect the K-pop track selected for the *Star Power*
    performance in Scene Nine, as determined by each production.

2. 아이고 AIGO. A Korean exclamation expressing surprise, frustration, exhaustion, sympathy,
    or affection. Like 'oh no,' 'oh dear,' or even a deep sigh, depending on tone. It's commonly
    used by older generations and carries a lot of emotional nuances—it can be dramatic, comic,
    or deeply heartfelt.

She pulls on cotton work gloves, not looking at HANNAH.

HANNAH: Are you okay?

UMMA: [*Looking up at the fridge*] Oh … You … English? [*Unfazed*] Okay. Good thank you. 큰일 났어! 이 망할 거 불타고 있어! *keunil natseo! i manghal geo bultago isseo!* (The bloody thing is on fire!)

HANNAH: Is it on fire?

UMMA *gives the thumbs up, still not looking at* HANNAH.

UMMA: Yes, good!

HANNAH: [*raising her voice to be heard over the TV*] No, it's bad.

UMMA: Spam? Oh—yes. Buy two get one free!

HANNAH: What?

HANNAH *switches TV off.*

Pffffffft poooft! BAD SMOKE!

The fridge exhales more smoke. UMMA *laughs, not easing* HANNAH*'s concern.*

UMMA: Ha! No like smoke? Be with you soon.

She takes a fan from her pocket and flaps it, trying to blow the smoke away. Completing her transformation into human canary.

HANNAH: Should I call the fire people? [*Fire engine sound*] Wee-Orr-Wee-Orr!

UMMA: [*more celebratory than alarmed*] Wee-Orr! Wee-Orr! Bye-bye smoke.

She blows more air.

Poooft poooft. It's fixed.

The fridge light flickers. UMMA *bangs it with her fist. It stops.*

I fix.

Takes off her gloves and gives herself a big round of applause.

Okay. How can I help you?

She sees HANNAH*'s face for the first time.*

아이고!! *AIGO!!* (Oh my!!)

HANNAH: It's me. Hannah.

UMMA: I know.

UMMA *suddenly remembers her manners, overcorrecting.*

안녕하세요. *Annyeonghaseyo.* (Hello.)

HANNAH: [*nervously aborting Korean mid-word*] Annyeong-ha-*hello.*

> HANNAH *reaches up to hug* UMMA, *who remains on the ladder but it's too awkward.* UMMA *pats her on the head. Still perched above,* UMMA *gives a small, self-conscious bow.* HANNAH *mirrors it from below.* UMMA *begins her dismount.*

Let me help you.

> UMMA *shoos* HANNAH*'s hand away, instead using the fridge to steady herself.*

UMMA: Everything … a mess.

> *She tries to clean up but there's too much to do.*

HANNAH: It's great. Guess you need a new fridge?

UMMA: Why? Still work good.

> *She takes out a small plastic stool from behind the counter and hands* HANNAH *a bottle of water from the fridge.*

Sit. Sit. Down.

HANNAH: Oh, it's okay, I've got some water.

UMMA: [*ignoring her*] See? Fridge. Cold. You want banana milk? Juice? Cola?

> *She hands* HANNAH *one of every drink.*

HANNAH: [*nervous rambling*] Thank you. Everything is so cute—even the Spam. Do shops in Korea always stack it like a mountain?

> *Beat.*

Mount Spam-erest.

> UMMA *offers a polite laugh, the kind usually reserved for unstable people.*

[*Struggling but trying*] 다시 보게 돼서 기뻐요. *Dashi boge dwaeseo gippeoyo.* (I'm glad we got to see each other again.)

UMMA: Is that Korean?

HANNAH: Yeah, I was trying to say, I'm glad … dashi … It's good to see you again.

UMMA: Better you speak English.

> *Beat.*

HANNAH: So, this is your mart! Can't believe I'm finally here. Oh my god, we should get a selfie.

UMMA: [*dry, matter of fact*] No selfie thank you.

HANNAH: You're right, I probably look like a mess. I'm all sweaty.

UMMA: Why you wear coat in summer?

HANNAH: I was just trying to look a bit less … long-haul flight.

She starts touring the mart, still holding the drinks.

Gosh, from your messages, I was expecting it would be just snacks and drinks, but you've got socks and sunglasses and spaghetti!

UMMA: A big new mart open near me, so, I have to … How you say? Sell more things. My customers like.

HANNAH *tours the mart, drinks still in hand.*

HANNAH: Oh yeah, I can see it's all very *convenient* … I got a bit lost in the alleyway trying to find my way here. The taxi dropped me off near a night club.

She stares into the fridge, wishing she could put the bottles down.

UMMA: You want beer?

HANNAH: I'm good, I've got enough liquids. Actually, there were heaps of drunk kids around. Or maybe they were adults. Everyone looks so young in Korea.

UMMA *points to the drinks.*

UMMA: You don't want drinks?

HANNAH *is afraid of disappointing her.*

HANNAH: I'm happy to hold them.

UMMA *takes the drinks from* HANNAH *and catches sight of her reflection in the fridge.*

UMMA: [*to herself*] Aigo!

She whips off her visor and presses down her broccoli-like perm.

HANNAH: My flight was delayed, I didn't mean to get here so late.

UMMA: You here a week early.

HANNAH: [*taking out her iPhone*] What?

The electric doorbell 'DING DONGS' alerting UMMA *to a delivery arriving.*

UMMA: [*shouting at the door at offstage delivery person*] 늦었잖아! 하루 종일 기다렸어요! 아직 신선해야 돼 되요! *Neujeotjanha! haru jongil gidaryeosseo! Ajik sinsunhaeya dwae!* (You're late! I've been waiting all day! It better still be fresh!)

HANNAH: You get deliveries at midnight?

UMMA: Seoul does not sleep.

> UMMA *goes to get the delivery.*

HANNAH: What time do you close?

> UMMA *points back to a faded sign as she exits.*

Twenty-four-hour convenience mart.

> UMMA *enters with the box.*

UMMA: Not twenty-four. Shh … FAKE news. I close mart. Sleep five hours.

HANNAH: Wow. That must be hard.

UMMA: No, just work. Why you here? You message say, you come next week.

HANNAH: [*showing her iPhone*] I know I didn't give you much warning, but remember, I said … some *things* had … changed … and look, yeah, I said Saturday—

UMMA: No, you come next Saturday.

HANNAH: Maybe it didn't translate properly. I can go to a hotel.

UMMA: Okay.

HANNAH: Would it be better if I come back *next* Saturday?

UMMA: Okay.

HANNAH: Cool … well, I'll see next week. Bye.

> *Beat.* HANNAH *awkwardly grabs her suitcase. She walks away but* UMMA *stops her.*

UMMA: No. No. I fix.

> *She reboots, suddenly switching tones.*

Go back.

HANNAH: What?

> UMMA *straightens.*

UMMA: I'm ready. Go again. Walk in mart.

HANNAH, *not exactly sure what is going on but plays along and walks back into the mart.*

HANNAH: Surprise! I'm back.

UMMA: WELCOME TO KOREA!

She bows.

안녕! *Annyeong!* (Hello!) You look … not same as last time.

HANNAH: [*joking*] Older? Ha ha.

UMMA: [*not joking*] Yes.

HANNAH: It's only been a year—

UMMA: How you say? The sun very strong in Australia.

HANNAH: Oh yeah …

UMMA: We look like sisters!

HANNAH *laughs at the 'joke' but* UMMA *isn't joking.*

HANNAH: When I show people photos of you, they say you look too young to be my mother.

Beat.

UMMA: You come to Seoul for summer vacation?

HANNAH: I guess it's not really a holiday. No, so we can spend a chunk … I mean a long time … *all* of the summer with you.

UMMA: But you have good job in Sydney?

HANNAH: Yeah … I work in the arts.

UMMA: [*horrified*] You have NO JOB?!

HANNAH: I'm freelance, which means … I have a lot of free time.

UMMA: I have to work in mart.

HANNAH *has a quiet determination—the kind that sees possibility where others see only endings.*

HANNAH: That's cool, I can be your assistant. And, when we're not working … day off … we can vacation, like tourists … We can hire hanboks. Hike the mountains … not Spam Mountain … Namsan Mountain … Can we go to the palace?

UMMA: I don't have day off. I work all the days. I think you only come for a small time.

HANNAH: Yeah, but then I said … [*Reading phone*] I haven't been to Korea in the summer before …

She scrolls through her phone, showing UMMA *the messages.*

Maybe I could stay with you? Our messages … see—you said … *okay.*

UMMA *doesn't even look at the phone. She starts stress-polishing a garden gnome.*

UMMA: Shhh.

HANNAH: I think there's been a mix-up.

UMMA: You be more happy if you go on vacation. Go to Busan, eat fish.

HANNAH: No, I want to be with you. I think this is my bad, I confused things. But look, I'm here now. And I don't mind working here.

UMMA *launches into a very animated tirade.*

UMMA: 당신이 내 가게에서 일하는 데 내가 동의하는 이유는 무엇입니까? *Dangsin-i nae gageeseo ilhaneun de naega dong-uihaneun iyuneun mueos-ibnikka?* (Why would I agree for you to work in my shop?)

HANNAH: Do you mind speaking a bit slower?

UMMA: 나는 이것이 실수라는 것을 알았습니다. *Naneun igeos-i silsulaneun geos-eul al-assseubnida.* (I knew this was a mistake.)

HANNAH: Did you just say … mistake? Hang on, I've got this translation app. You speak into it like this … [*To phone*] I've missed you.

PHONE: [*loudspeaker*] *Bo-go ship-eoss-eo-yo. Han-guk-e dol-aon ge jeong-mal haeng-bok-hae-yo.* (I've missed you.)

It's impossible to tell how UMMA *feels about what has been translated.* HANNAH *tries to hand her iPhone to* UMMA.

HANNAH: Here, you try.

UMMA: No. My English. Good. You. Korean … Bad.

HANNAH: I've been trying to learn. I can hear way better than I can read.

UMMA *picks up a persimmon from the counter and speaks quickly.*

UMMA: What I say? 이 감은 얼마예요? *I gam-eun eolmayeyo?* (How much is this persimmon?)

HANNAH: Um …

UMMA: Aigo!

HANNAH *speaks into her phone but her Korean is bad.*

HANNAH: 한국어 실력이 점점 좋아지고 있어요. *Hanguk-eo sillyeog-i jeomjeom joh-ajigo iss-eoyo.* (My Korean skills are getting better.)

HANNAH's *stilted pronunciation confuses the translation app.*

PHONE: [*loudspeaker*] MY KOREAN SKILLS ARE GRADUALLY BOILING.

HANNAH: Oh no, that's not right.

UMMA: You … no no no work in my mart. Koreans. How you say? You. From Australia.

HANNAH: Foreign? Oh yeah, Koreans don't like foreigners? Well, technically I'm Korean.

UMMA: No.

HANNAH: I was born here.

UMMA: Not the same.

HANNAH: You can explain to them I'm your—

UMMA: Hannah not Korean!

> HANNAH *tries to hold back tears.* UMMA *has never been confronted by her crying child before.*

You cry?

HANNAH: I'm fine.

UMMA: Stop.

HANNAH: It's the fridge smoke.

> HANNAH *pats her eyes.*

UMMA: Customers see … Stop. You go now. Vacation more, happy for Hannah.

HANNAH: I want to get to know you—

UMMA: I—I … I don't want you—

HANNAH: You don't want me?

UMMA: 아이고, 그게 아니야. *Aigo, geuge aniya.* (Aigo, that's not what I am saying.)

HANNAH: I can't go back to Sydney.

UMMA: No cry. You stay here.

HANNAH: Are you sure?

> *Beat.*

UMMA: Okay.

HANNAH: Does that mean, yes?

> *Beat.*

UMMA: You must be hungry?

She grabs some ramyun from the shelf and fills it with hot water. HANNAH watches as she delicately tears open the zigzagged edge of a small sachet of seasoning. The moment the boiling water meets the noodles, a sizzle erupts. UMMA shuffles back with the apology noodles on a tray and hands it to HANNAH with some metal chopsticks from below the counter.

UMMA turns the television back on and returns to work. Music plays in the background.

HANNAH: I like Butter. The song playing ... and the grocery item. I love BTS.

UMMA: They have K-pop in Australia?

HANNAH: Yeah, of course, BTS are like the biggest boy band in the world.

UMMA shuffles back with the apology noodles.

Thank you.

UMMA: Eat.

HANNAH opens the lid of her noodles.

Not now. Not cooked. Wait.

HANNAH: Ooh, nice gnome.

She absentmindedly reaches out to touch the gnome. UMMA moves it away without a word.

Oh god, there's another one ... oh, more gnomes up there too.

She looks out the back.

Is there garden out the back?

UMMA: No. Storeroom.

HANNAH: Do you sell many gnomes?

UMMA: No.

HANNAH: I've worked in the retail sector. I'm just trying to get a feel for the store layout, the product placement ... visual hierarchy ...

HANNAH goes back to her noodles, she tries to pick them up, but they keep slipping through her chopsticks. She adjusts her grip, fumbling, determined. There's something quietly sad about it—a Korean girl struggling with something so small, so instinctive.

Whoopsie! Korean metal chopsticks are so slippery. I'm like a panda—prefer bamboo.

UMMA, *still working, steals a glance. For a moment, guilt flickers across her face. She should have been the one to teach* HANNAH *this—how to hold them. She almost says something, almost reaches out, but instead, she turns away.*

HANNAH: [*abandoning her noodles*] I've been employee of the month. When I was at uni, I was a sandwich artist. Does Korea have Subway?

UMMA: Big train?

HANNAH: No, big bread roll. I could make a foot-long ham sub in under a minute.

UMMA: Okay. Drunk customers be here soon. You show me work. Me. Customer. Go!

UMMA *goes to the fridge and grabs some banana milk.* HANNAH *realises she is mid-job interview and goes behind the counter.*

안녕하세요. *Annyeonghaseyo.* (Hello.)

HANNAH: [*not as fluent*] Ann-yeong-ha-seyo.

HANNAH *fluffs around with a plastic bag.*

UMMA: 봉투 괜찮아요. *Bongtu gwaenchanayo.* (It's okay, I don't need a bag.)

HANNAH *places the banana milk in a bag.* UMMA *gives some cash from her pocket to* HANNAH. *She runs over to the fridge to check the price and comes back almost knocking the lucky cat off the counter.*

HANNAH: Ah … that will be … five hundred won. Um … how do I … ?

She presses a button and receipt starts printing.

Whoopsie … Ah, here we go.

She presses something that opens the register.

Oh … there's not a lot of enough change. I'll have to give you coins.

She hands UMMA *a handful of coins—like she's emptied a child's piggy bank.*

UMMA: Aigo!

HANNAH: Gam-sa-hamnida. Thank you.

Beat.

Did I get the job?

UMMA: [*looking at the coins*] Wrong money. You can't count.

HANNAH: There wasn't enough in the float.

UMMA: Float?

HANNAH: Like, cha-ching …

She does the 'makes it rain' hand gesture.

Cash. Money.

UMMA *dumps the coins back in the register and cleans up the mess on the counter.*

UMMA: You can't speak Korean.

HANNAH: I'm just a bit nervous—

UMMA: I have lots of tourist customers. My English. Good. And I watch HBO.

HANNAH: I've watched *Squid Game*, without the subtitles.

UMMA: Everyone has watched *Squid Game*. 아이씨 *Aish!*[3] Why you not learn Korean from TV?

HANNAH: I … I've tried to learn Korean. I did some classes but … Look, maybe if I work here in the mart, my Korean will get better? Look, this has all been very weird.

UMMA: Weird?

HANNAH: Like … not what we were both expecting.

UMMA: I know what weird is. This is very weird.

HANNAH: Should we just start again … *again?*

HANNAH *exits. The electric door dings. She wheels straight back in.*

Hello. I know we don't know each other that well. But I was very good at making foot-long bread rolls, and … to be honest, I can't afford a hotel.

UMMA: You want to stay here? Work here?

HANNAH: I really want to get to know you … and learn about the rest of my family. My grandmother—she worked here, right? My father.

---

3. 아이씨 AISH is a Korean exclamation used to express frustration, annoyance, or mild anger—kind of like 'ugh,' 'damn,' or 'argh' in English.

I know they're not alive anymore but I'm hoping you can tell me about them too … and, like, Korean stuff. I've only been here once, to meet you … and yeah … that was just a quick trip, so, I dunno, maybe you can even teach me how to make kimchi?

UMMA: Kimchi in fridge.

HANNAH: Well, it's more like *smoked* kimchi ha ha.

> UMMA *doesn't laugh.*

Can we just … give it a try?

UMMA: Okay.

> *Although* UMMA *doesn't explicitly agree,* HANNAH *hears what she wants to hear.*

HANNAH: Okay? I can stay. Good. Yes. Thank you … What can I do?

UMMA: Go to bed.

HANNAH: Great.

> HANNAH *awkwardly stands with her suitcase unsure where to go.*

UMMA: My apartment upstairs.

> UMMA *gestures toward the door.* HANNAH *hesitates, then heads upstairs, dragging her suitcase behind her. As soon as she's out of sight,* UMMA *exhales shakily, crossing her arms. She takes a few steps, almost pacing, then stops herself. She pats a gnome on the counter, adjusting it with care, as if seeking reassurance. Absentmindedly, putting her visor back on, she turns on the TV behind the counter and flicks over to her favourite cable channel. The sound of four American women chatting over lunch fills the space. She sighs, letting the familiar voices settle around her. But her gaze turns distant, unfocused. The comfort doesn't take. She blinks, exhales, turns off the TV, tucks the mart into bed and heads upstairs.*

SCENE TWO

A week later.

The light shifts. Day folds into night. Hours blur and repeat. It's early—caught between the moon's sleep and the sun's rise. In the stillness, something new awakes.

HANNAH, *now in relaxed clothes, looks like an intruder—sneaking around in the dark, someone who doesn't quite fit here, but who is trying to earn her place. She works quickly, her former retail skills on display—efficient, methodical.*

UMMA *enters the shop, a pink Velcro roller protruding from her forehead like a rhinoceros horn. Bright lipstick, neatly drawn. Her ajumma style remains—bold, floral, practical—but today, there's a small upgrade. A quilted vest, fitted just so, and on her chest, a faux Chanel brooch. Less like she's bracing for an outdoor adventure, more considered.*

For years, her morning ritual has stayed the same. She moves through the darkness, the cool glow of the refrigerators lighting her way. Behind the counter, she flips a switch. Music fills the air—a whimsical melody, part children's TV show, part arcade game. She begins her workout. Knees rising, arms swinging, perfect sync. National Gymnastics.[4] The quiet discipline of ajumma exercise.

HANNAH: [*popping up from behind a shelf*] MORNING!

> UMMA *screams. She fumbles for the light switch, grabbing the nearest weapon—an economy pack of toilet paper. The fluorescents flicker to life—her frantic gaze locking onto the intruder.*

UMMA: AHHHHHHHHHHHHHHHH!!!

> UMMA *whacks* HANNAH *with the toilet paper.* HANNAH's *nose starts bleeding.*

Oh! No! No!

---

4.   국민체조 NATIONAL GYMNASTICS was introduced in 1977 as a South Korean national fitness program, promoting health and discipline through simple, rhythmic exercises. Practised in schools, workplaces, and parks, it became a daily ritual, blending routine, resilience, and communal spirit.

UMMA flaps around, scrambling to turn the music off.

HANNAH: It's fine. I've got a sensitive schnoz. Used to get nosebleeds all the time when I was little.

UMMA grabs a cool pouch drink from the fridge and pushes it into HANNAH's nose.

HANNAH: Ow!

UMMA: I forget. Normally just me who live in mart.

HANNAH: I've been here for a week!

With surgical precision, UMMA grabs a pair of sunglasses and slaps them onto HANNAH's face, securing the pouch drink like an emergency ice pack.

UMMA: I fix.

HANNAH: Ohhhh.

She sighs with relief.

This works quite well. Wow, could've used this as a kid. Where have you been all my life … Anyway, I got up early. Ta-dah!

HANNAH gestures proudly at her newly arranged display—eager for approval.

I know, I know … You want me to stay out the back. BUT … I wanted to help. So, I put all the kitchen stuff here, the gloves and socks over there. And I hope you don't mind, but I moved the persimmons with the other fruit. At Subway, I oversaw the cookie display cabinet. Not to brag, but I do have a bit of a natural talent for visual merchandising. I've noticed most of your customers just buy one thing, but if they see all the products nicely grouped together, they might spend a little extra.

Beat. UMMA surveys everything. Unreadable.

I've been planning it all week. Got up early. Wanted to surprise you. *And,* I've already mopped the floors.

UMMA: Okay.

HANNAH: TA-DAH! I put all the garden gnomes together, like one big happy family. Do you like it?

UMMA: Aigo.

HANNAH tries to sound casual, but eager.

HANNAH: I've been getting the hang of the mart. Maybe I could even help you run it one day!

UMMA: You work in Sydney doing The Arts.

UMMA hovers near the gnomes, caught between politeness, having just injured her daughter, and the overwhelming urge to move the gnomes. Her hands twitch slightly, resisting the urge to rearrange. She eyes them with restrained disapproval.

HANNAH *doesn't mean to offend, but is obviously privileged.*

HANNAH: Yeah, but it's kind of fun for me … playing shop. Well, not playing … It's just nice to do a real job again.

UMMA: You go back out to stockroom.

UMMA starts the music again and tries to resume her squats. HANNAH lingers.

HANNAH: I interrupted your yoga.

UMMA: National exercise routine. All Koreans learn at school. We do every morning.

She exercises. HANNAH takes off the sunglasses and ice-cream combo.

HANNAH: You know we have a similar thing in Australia. At school, we learn the Nutbush. I'll show you.

She starts demonstrating.

Church house, gin house …

UMMA: What is this?

HANNAH: Knee, knee, / knee, knee.

UMMA: Time to start work.

HANNAH: You keep going. I really shouldn't have Nutbushed.

UMMA turns off the music and opens the mart. She starts separating the garden gnomes, returning them to their original places.

UMMA: Hannah, better if you go on vacation. Train to Busan only take three hour. Great fish.

HANNAH: You don't like the gnomes … together?

UMMA: Not the same.

HANNAH: Yeah, but don't you think they're better together? Like a little family?

UMMA: No.

A sound at the front door. UMMA *springs into action.*

Go. Customer.

UMMA *pushes* HANNAH *behind the sunglasses stand.*

HANNAH: What are you doing?

UMMA: Shh … Oh, just delivery.

UMMA *shuffles off. She thanks the delivery person and returns with a heavy box.*

HANNAH: You don't want to be seen with me?

UMMA: I work good—just me. You be happy on Busan vacation. Eat crabs.

HANNAH: I try to help, but you don't let me do anything. There's only so many times I can dust the toilet paper in the storeroom.

UMMA *looks at the delivery box in front of her. It's heavy. She eyes* HANNAH, *hesitates, and almost asks—then stops herself.*

UMMA: Aigo!

HANNAH *watches her struggle for a moment, then instinctively reaches for the box.*

HANNAH: Here, let me—

UMMA *snaps, yanking the box away just in time.*

UMMA: No!

There's an awkward silence as UMMA *hoists the box with great effort.*

HANNAH: Okay, but, for the record, this would be easier if you let me—

UMMA: Shh. No record.

HANNAH: Maybe if we just got out of the / mart.

UMMA: Korea, we work hard and no … no … How you say? You don't get Korean way.

UMMA *waddles away with the box, muttering under her breath.* HANNAH *disappears up the stairs to the apartment.* UMMA, *disgruntled, begins putting everything back in its place. A moment later,* HANNAH *returns—suitcase in hand.*

HANNAH: I'm going.

UMMA: Where?

HANNAH: Back to Sydney. You don't want me here.

UMMA: My mart is real. Not for child to play in. Mart is my life.

HANNAH: Just forget the mart for a second.

> *Beat. A last ditch effort:*

What do you do for fun? Do you like cats or dogs? Is pink your favourite colour? Do red beans make your tummy hurt? Every year on my birthday … I thought about you.

> *Beat.*

Were you thinking about me too?

> *Beat.* UMMA *stills, unmoving.*

I came here … I thought—what? You know my boyfriend said this was—

UMMA: You have a boyfriend?

HANNAH: We broke up.

UMMA: You didn't come for us? You had nowhere to go?

HANNAH: It's not like that … I was already coming here.

UMMA: [*escalating*] Fake news! [*To gnome*] 애가 나를 속였네. *Eh-ga na-reul so-gyeot-neh.* (She's betrayed, fooled me?)

> UMMA *turns, moves a garden gnome back into its place, hands shaking slightly.*

HANNAH: Just—put the gnome down!

UMMA: 네가 나한테 어떻게 이럴수 있니? *Nega nahante eotteoke ireol su inni?* (How can you do this to me?)

HANNAH: Can you speak to me in English!

UMMA: No, you speak to me in Korean!

> HANNAH *steps back, dragging her suitcase away to the door.*

HANNAH: You know what? This was a huge mistake. I shouldn't have come back.

UMMA: 가지마! 가지마! *Gajima! Gajima!* (Don't go! Don't go!)

> UMMA *speaks out song lyrics,[5] desperate, grasping for words she can't find on her own.*

---

5. The lyrics are scripted dialogue and do not need to be substituted with actual songs unless a production chooses to do so. However, any lyrics used should reflect the themes and intentions outlined in the script.

UMMA: The shape ... The shape ... of ... your eyes ... the shadow of you—

> Girl, I need a minute—To sort out what's real, what's just a blur.

HANNAH *freezes. She turns slowly.* UMMA *is fully committed now.*

> Some days, you make me feel like I'm losing it.
> Some days, I swear you don't even like me, like ... uh.
> I need air, I need space, I need to step away—
> Because I need to know ... Who are you?

Long beat.

HANNAH: Did you just talk to me in ... *K-pop*?
UMMA: Yes.

Beat.

HANNAH: Disco tears, in a cereal bowl. Sold my secrets to a dancing troll.
UMMA: Ice cream, with a jelly bean. No chill with my slippers on.
BOTH: Ping ping, message on my screen.

> Mango juice and a claw machine, huh.

UMMA *and* HANNAH *gain momentum.*

HANNAH: Feel the sparkle rising—
UMMA: Can you see the sun eyes?
HANNAH: I'm shining.
UMMA: Wa-o-oh!

HANNAH *and* UMMA *stare hard at each other.*

> Your favourite BTS member. Jungkook? Or Jimin?

They both point at a different BTS member.

BOTH: Suga! WAAHHH!

They both cautiously start doing BTS choreography together.

[*Singing*] Sent my ex a glitter toad, confetti sky, don't need no guy.
I'm fire—I want to GLOW! GLOW-uh-Oh!

SCENE THREE

The next day.

UMMA *has finally given* HANNAH *a real job. Side by side, they stack ramyun cups on a shelf. Each time* HANNAH *places one,* UMMA *quietly nudges it into a different position.*

HANNAH: Do you wanna see me tap dance?

UMMA: [*matter-of-fact*] No.

HANNAH: But, I won the twelve-years-and-under Song and Dance Championship at the Lake Macquarie Dance Eisteddfod.

UMMA: IS—Tedd … ?

HANNAH: Eis—tedd—fod. It's like competitions for children. You dress up, sing your little heart out, win a plastic trophy and lifelong trauma.

UMMA: [*impressed*] Wah!

HANNAH: I had this unbeatable routine. Dani Lock was my main competition. But when she saw me side-stage in my black fishnets and a bowler hat, she'd shit her leotard. Ring the bell.

> UMMA *frowns.*

UMMA: Oh?

HANNAH: [*announcer voice, dramatic flourish*] Ding ding! Competitor number five, performing 'All That Jazz'!

> HANNAH *jazz-walks into position and launches into a Fosse-inspired song and tap routine. She finishes with a flourish. Panting, waiting for applause.*

And that's when the audience would clap.

> UMMA *does not applaud.*

I won a massive trophy, even bigger than that gnome.

UMMA: You sing about jazz and then do tap dance?

HANNAH: It was a very good routine. Mum took me to all my dance classes and eisteddfods on weekends. But she wasn't a stage mum or anything like that she was more of a … dance mum.

UMMA: How are they different?

HANNAH: Dance mums coach from the wings, and stage mums, well ... they do too. Actually, they're both kind of insane. But we had fun, it was our thing and we had matching jackets.

UMMA: And fishnet. Aish! Too ... sexy for girl only twelve?

HANNAH: There were sequins on the leotard to make it look like a corset. I wasn't actually wearing lingerie.

UMMA: [*flat, unimpressed*] Bad. I don't like.

HANNAH: [*defensive*] Mum made my costume. Took her weeks to sequin it.

UMMA: [*backpedalling*] Oh—yes, sparkle look, very pretty.

HANNAH: She was really proud of me when I won.

UMMA: Yes. Yes. She did a good job.

    Beat. HANNAH *not wanting to lose her new connection with* UMMA.

HANNAH: How do you know all the BTS dance moves?

UMMA: Internet. I learn at night when there are no customers.

HANNAH: Why don't you close earlier?

UMMA: My mum wanted it this way.

HANNAH: [*careful*] Was she strict? Hard? Or, um ... soft?

UMMA: Hard like fruit. Even when she got old. Never soft.

    UMMA *busies herself. The silence sits heavy.*

HANNAH: Did you ever imagine me tap-dancing in Australia?

UMMA: [*avoiding eye contact*] No one tell me where baby go. I don't know until we meet last year that they give my baby to Australia.

HANNAH: No one told you.

    She processes.

Where did you think I went?

UMMA: I don't think about it. [*Then, to gnome*] 여기는 네 집 아니야, 꼬마야. *Yeogineun ne jip aniya, kkomaya.* (This isn't your home, little one.)

    UMMA *moves the gnome back to its usual position.*

HANNAH: You really like the gnomes, don't you?

UMMA: They are my friends. Gnomes not for sale.

    Beat.

It's late. Go to bed.

HANNAH: No. I'm not tired.
UMMA: I would never say no to my umma.
HANNAH: What would she have done?

UMMA *gives her a look. Nothing more needs to be said.*

HANNAH: Okay. Goodnight.
UMMA: [*keeping up facade, lightly*] Sleep well.
HANNAH: Tomorrow, let's go out—
UMMA: [*pushing* HANNAH *along*] Okay … Bye bye.

HANNAH *exits. The moment she's gone,* UMMA*'s performance drops. She slumps over the counter. Finally, alone. The relief of a mother at the end of a long day. She goes to get a healthy snack but immediately switches to a treat. Turtle Chips.*

HANNAH *sneaks back in, like a toddler out of bed.*

HANNAH: [*whining, small voice*] I can't sleep.
UMMA: Aigo!
HANNAH: [*whinging, extra pitiful*] I'm hungry.

UMMA *sighs, holding up the bag of Turtle Chips.*

UMMA: K-snack? Turtle Chip?
HANNAH: Yay!

HANNAH *climbs onto the counter. Feet swinging like a child.* UMMA *hands her a Turtle Chip.*

UMMA: [*stern, but fond*] Five minutes. Then bed.
HANNAH: Mmm … ten.
UMMA: [*warning look*] Five.
HANNAH: [*fake groan, dramatic*] Ugh. Fiiiine.

UMMA *looks at the time on her phone.*

UMMA: WAH! I miss the start!

UMMA *flicks on the TV. A colourful Korean reality/talent show can be heard but not seen by the audience.*

TV: 우리의 첫 번째 참가자들입니다 … 시애틀에서 온 자매 팀! *Uriui cheot beonjjae chamgajadeul-imnida … Siaeteul-eseo on jamae tim!* (Our first contestants tonight … a sister team from Seattle!)
TV: [*American girl*] Hello Seoul! We're singing sisters from Seattle. We have Starbucks … but do we have *Star Power*?

HANNAH: Like for amateurs?

UMMA: Sadder your life, the more chance you win. You need … something make you, wow!

HANNAH: Unique?

UMMA: Yes. Last week winner, he sing with a dog woofing. Judges cry, oh—he so cute but dog not even sing right notes.

HANNAH: Oh, we have reality TV shows like this is Australia.

UMMA: *Star Power* is famous K-TV show.

HANNAH: So, what, you just add a K in front of anything and it becomes Korean?

UMMA: Yes. K-pop. K-drama. K-beauty. K-film. K-food.

HANNAH: [*teasing*] K—Hannah?

UMMA: Not for human.

HANNAH: I know, it was a / joke.

UMMA: [*gesturing to the gnomes*] Shh. Others in cinema.

HANNAH: Are garden gnomes traditional in Korean culture? K-gnome?

UMMA: No, but they make them here so gnome is Korean.

HANNAH: But, if I put that K-gnome in my garden in Sydney?

UMMA: She is my gnome.

HANNAH: Yeah, but what if I just took her home? I think she'd like to live there.

UMMA: Gnome would miss me.

HANNAH: Maybe she would forget the mart?

UMMA: Just because you move somewhere new, you don't forget your home.

> *Beat. They sit together, watching, crunching, quiet.* Star Power *contestants sing in the background.*

When I was girl, I used to sing for my umma. Just there, next to grapes. I want to be a singer.

HANNAH: What? Really?

UMMA: The teacher pick me to sing 'Arirang'[6] at the Independence Day ceremony.

HANNAH: What's 'Arirang'?

---

6. 'ARIRANG' is a traditional Korean folk song with no known individual composer, dating back over six hundred years. As such, it exists in the public domain and may be used freely. However, modern arrangements or specific recordings may still be subject to copyright.

UMMA: All Koreans know, very famous song.

HANNAH: The national anthem?

UMMA: No. More special … heart song. I want to be a singer. But my umma say not a real job. I have to work at mart.

She turns back to the television.

This group. Can't sing. Only on *Star Power* because they are pretty. Very Korean look even though they from America.

HANNAH: What's a Korean look?

UMMA *is careful not to look at* HANNAH's *face.*

UMMA: See, she … straight eyebrows. You … round. White skin. Not brown. Thin … not … Clothes cute … not … How you say? Not like … opp … opp …

HANNAH: Opposite?

UMMA: Yes. Opposite of you.

She smiles—not a criticism, just a fact.

HANNAH: I wish I had a K-look.

UMMA: You want?

HANNAH: Yeah, but you're right. I don't think I have the right / look.

UMMA: 완전 호박꽃이네. *Wanjeon hobak-kkot-ine.* (She looks like a pumpkin.)

HANNAH: 호박 *Hobak?*

UMMA: Pumpkin.

HANNAH: Pumpkin?

UMMA: She looks like pumpkin.

HANNAH: Koreans are so harsh.

UMMA: Here you must fit in. Not good to stand out.

She clears her throat.

[*In American accent*] '*We all judge. That's our hobby.*'

She laughs then yells at screen.

I give NO points to American singing pumpkins!

HANNAH: So, foreigners can go on *Star Power*?

Beat.

We should enter.

UMMA: Huh?

HANNAH: Come on, we could totally do that.

UMMA: We have no talent.

HANNAH: Excuse me, I'm a tap-dancing champion and you wanted to be a singer.

UMMA: [*turning back to the television*] That was long time ago.

HANNAH: So? It could be fun.

UMMA: [*waving her off, firm*] I have work.

HANNAH: But you have time to learn K-pop dances at night. Oh my god, can you imagine the opening montage. '*She crossed oceans ... faced her past ... and now she's here ... ready to debut. One adoptee. One mother. One mart. One shot at stardom.*'

UMMA: AIGO!

> HANNAH *types on her phone.*

HANNAH: First round, you just fill out a form. Second round is a video audition. Then boom! You're a contestant on *Star Power*. Whoa! You didn't tell me first prize is twenty million won.

UMMA: Yes, new winner every week.

HANNAH: That's over—

> *Uses her fingers to calculate.*

Twenty grand.

UMMA: Time for you to go to bed.

> HANNAH *manically taps and raps with a mimed microphone.*

HANNAH: No sleep, no rest, grind all night, burning bright like neon lights. Step by step, we take the throne. Work so hard, take the crown home!

> *Beat.*

UMMA: That was weird.

HANNAH: You mean, *unique.* We could be the first tap-dancing K-pop band. Come on, let's just do it. Can you fill out the application? It needs to be in Korean.

UMMA: I have to work.

HANNAH: Look, we probably won't even make it past the first round but it's just something fun we can do *together.* We can make up our own dances when there's no customers. Think of it as staff development, team building.

UMMA: No.

HANNAH: All we do is work.

UMMA: I'm busy with mart.

HANNAH: Is anything more important to you than the mart?

UMMA: No.

HANNAH: What about me?

UMMA: Why would I go on TV with you?!

> UMMA *suddenly turns away, back to her gnomes.*

HANNAH: Just forget it. You're right, it's a stupid idea.

> *Beat.*

UMMA: You still hungry?

HANNAH: No.

> HANNAH *stares at the television, using the talent show as a shield.*

UMMA: [*trying to redirect*] You think they are couple?

> HANNAH *doesn't respond.*

Oh—no, he look so old.

> *Beat.*

I think he's her father.

> *Beat.*

His voice is nice … but his body is fat.

> *Beat.*

HANNAH: Do you ever wonder … if things had been different?

> UMMA *keeps her eyes on the screen, but she's not really watching.*

Maybe we'd be working in the mart together, like we are now.

> UMMA *adjusts the TV's volume as if the show's audio suddenly matters, forcing their conversation a few decibels louder.*

UMMA: Judges about to score.

HANNAH: Did my father look like me?

UMMA: Way past your bedtime.

HANNAH: I'm not tired.

> UMMA*'s breath slightly unsteady.*

UMMA: You don't want to know who wins? Okay. We watch something else.

> UMMA *switches to her favourite cable channel. Four American women, chatting about men.*

HANNAH: Please—You've never talked about him.

UMMA: I watch this show every night, to learn English.

HANNAH: I know it must be hard. Can you just turn that off?

UMMA: [*rubbing her chest*] You don't want to watch? Okay … time for bed.

> HANNAH *grabs the remote and switches off the TV.*

HANNAH: My father—

UMMA: I … I don't remember.

HANNAH: I've never understood, it's not clear on my adoption papers, did he die before or after I was born?

UMMA: He … he … it was a long time ago.

> UMMA*'s breathing quickens. She looks away, gripping the edge of the counter.*

HANNAH: It doesn't make sense to me.

> *For a second, it looks like* UMMA *might speak. Instead, her breathing goes shallow.*
>
> *She suddenly gasps, clutching her chest.*

가슴이 답답해. 숨이 막혀. *Gaseumi dapdapae. Sumi makhyeo.* (My chest … I can't breathe.)

> UMMA *tries to steady herself, but her breath is shallow, fast— she's trapped, spiralling.*

HANNAH: Oh god, are you okay?

> UMMA *turns abruptly and rushes up the stairs to the apartment.* HANNAH *is left alone.*
>
> *Night exhales into morning. The air holds its breath.*

SCENE FOUR

Two days later.

HANNAH *enters and turns on the mart lights. The gnome on the counter, watching. Or waiting.* HANNAH *glances around to make sure she's alone. Then gently picks it up.*

HANNAH: [*quietly, to the gnome*] Why does she even have you?

> *She presses it to her chest like a child with a toy she doesn't understand but can't let go of. For a moment, she holds the gnome like it's hers. Like it might answer back. But before she can wait for an answer—she notices smoke rising from the fridge again. She moves without thinking, gives it a quick, expert hit. The smoke stops. The fridge hums back to life.*

> HANNAH *looks out at the world—unsure of where she belongs. If she leaves now, there may be nothing left to return to. If she stays? Just as uncertain. But instinctively, she knows—there's only one way forward. She sets the gnome down. Picks up a duster. And begins again.*

UMMA: [*yelling from offstage*] HANNAH! HANNAH!!

> UMMA *runs in, out of breath, holding her Samsung Galaxy.*

HANNAH: What's wrong?
UMMA: Next … round. Orrr … Orddd … shon.
HANNAH: Audition?
UMMA: Yes. Audition video. We need to send by tomorrow.
HANNAH: I don't understand.
UMMA: *Star Power.*
HANNAH: You applied?
UMMA: You don't like dusting toilet paper.
HANNAH: I thought you didn't want to—
UMMA: Not me. You! I apply for you. Eis-tedd-fod champion.

> *Animating her favourite gnome, in a gnome voice.*

'*Hannah come all the way from Sydney. She think you can win* Star Power.'

HANNAH: But why?

UMMA: [*still as gnome*] '*She want you to be happy.*' [*Her own voice*] I fix.

HANNAH: But … I'm not actually that good.

UMMA: I help you … how you say?

> *She goes into coach mode, claps.*

High note! Kick leg! Splits! Big smile! From the top!

HANNAH: You want to be my … coach?

UMMA: It will be fun. Something we can do *together.*

> *Beat.*

HANNAH: Well … if we are going to film an audition, we need better lighting.

> HANNAH *dims the lights.*

SCENE FIVE

Disco lights swirl around the mart. UMMA *has chosen a popular K-pop song[7] to use for the audition.*

UMMA: Five, six … five, six, seven, eight! RAP!!!

HANNAH: [*rapping, pronunciation shaky*] 불을 지펴 Bureul jipyeo (Light the fire) 내 잘못 아냐 Nae jalmos anya (It's not my fault)

UMMA: TAP!

HANNAH: [*tapping*] Bur … eul jip … yeo!

UMMA: [*correcting*] Bureul jipyeo!

HANNAH: [*not much better*] Bur … eul jip … yeo!

UMMA: [*like a drill sergeant*] RAP TAP! RAP TAP!

> HANNAH *bursts into a wild mash-up of tap-dancing and K-pop— rapid-fire heel taps crashing into body rolls, like Fred Astaire joining a K-pop band.*

HANNAH: Yeah, what, yeah, what. HA! Yeah yeah yeah, what what what—

UMMA: NUTBUSH!

> HANNAH *starts the Nutbush.*

---

7.   Invented K-pop lyrics. May be used as is or replaced with a licensed song depending on rights and production needs.

HANNAH: Ha, who runs this? Me! Girl, I run this! Kick that fear I run this. I run-run-run-run-run-run-run—

UMMA *turns off the disco lights.*

UMMA: STOP! [*Matter-of-fact*] You make me want to run.

HANNAH *stops, panting.*

HANNAH: Are you sure I shouldn't just do 'All That Jazz'?
UMMA: For *Star Power* audition? Aigo! I know what is best.
HANNAH: [*tries to rap again*] Bur … eul jip … yeo!
UMMA: You rap like a wet lettuce.
HANNAH: Well, if you're so good, you do it.
UMMA: [*coy*] I'm not that good. I'm just a shop owner.
HANNAH: GO! Oh, hang on, do it like we're on television.

She claps her hands like a slate board.

ACTION!

UMMA *doesn't move.*

ACTION means go.

UMMA *pretends to be shy, gets into position, then suddenly explodes into a confident, dramatic rap solo.*

UMMA: 불을 지펴 Bureul jipyeo (Light the fire)
내 잘못 아냐 Nae jalmos anya (It's not my fault)
내 길은 내가 정해 Nae gireun naega jeonghae (I choose my way)
울어도 웃어도 꺾이지 않아 Ureodo useodo kkeokkiji ana (Cry or laugh I don't break)
물어봐 / 싸워봐 Mureobwa ssawobwa (Bite back, flight back)
나는 깨어나 Naneun kkaeeona (I rise awake)
HANNAH: WOW!

She bursts into an enthusiastic round of applause.

UMMA: I know, I know, I'm very good. You do now, like me. ACTION!

They hear the 'DING DONG' of a delivery arriving. UMMA *shuffles out to get it.*

HANNAH: [*into her iPhone*] Ureodo useodo kkeokkiji ana.
PHONE: [*loudspeaker*] CRY OR LAUGH I DON'T BREAK.

UMMA *excitedly enters with a giant box.*

UMMA: WAH!!! HANNAH, YAH! 오늘은 진짜 행복한 날이야! *Oneureun jinjja haengbokan nariya!*

PHONE: [*loudspeaker*] TODAY IS A REALLY HAPPY DAY!

> UMMA *rips open the box. She takes out a huge haul of on-trend K-girl fashion.*

UMMA: Look what I buy for Hannah.

HANNAH: You got me new clothes?

UMMA: You want more Korean look!

> UMMA *passes* HANNAH *a new outfit.*

Put on now. ACTION!

> UMMA *waits until* HANNAH *is out of sight. She pulls out a stash of items, a hot glue gun and a few sparkly accessories. Finally, she reveals a sequinned bling cap. She tilts it just right, then checks her reflection in the fridge door. Turning to face the gnomes like a seasoned performer, she starts rapping.*

Yeah, what, yeah, what.
> HA! Yeah yeah yeah, what what what.
> Ha, who runs this? Me! Girl, I run this!
> Kick that fear I run this. I run-run-run-run-run-run-run.

> HANNAH *yells from upstairs, cutting off* UMMA'*s rap mid-flow.*

HANNAH: The skirt is very small.

UMMA: But I got you an extra-extra-large.

HANNAH: I'm ready!

UMMA: NO! NOT NOW.

> *She grabs a random item and pretends it's a microphone.*

Okay! [*In faux announcer voice*] Making her K-pop debut, introducing our new idol, Hannah!

> HANNAH *awkwardly emerges, tugging at the hem of her short pleated mini skirt and adjusting the sailor-collared shirt. She's clearly unsure about the outfit.*

WAH!!!

> *She enthusiastically applauds.*

Oh … you look amazing.

HANNAH: I look like a toddler who likes boats.

UMMA: Sexy, eh? You want to be on *Star Power*?

HANNAH: I can't dance in this, you'll see my bum.

UMMA: But you wear sequin-corset-for-All-That-Jazz-Eis-tedd-fod-dance? This is K-pop style.

HANNAH: It's not the same thing.

UMMA: [*disappointed*] I always do what my umma tell me to do.

HANNAH: [*reaching for the box*] I didn't mean to upset you. It's great, let me see the rest.

UMMA: I do all this for happy Hannah. [*To the gnome, sad*] 내가 해달라는 거 다 해줬는데도, 아직도 안 행복하대. *Naega haedallaneun geo da haejwonneundedo, ajikdo an haengbokhadae.* (I get her what she wants and she's still not happy.)

HANNAH: Wow. I've always wanted a tweed matching set. All of this would have been expensive.

UMMA: But you like? I like new K-Hannah.

HANNAH: You do?

UMMA: Very pretty.

> *She fires up her Samsung Galaxy.*

I want selfie! Say kimchi!

HANNAH: Kimchi!

UMMA: [*looking at the selfie*] WAH! This girl look like a winner to me.

HANNAH: But this is just the audition video. I'm not actually on the show yet.

UMMA: AISH! [*Bad New York accent*] Not with that attitude.

> *She winks. Her bling cap twinkles—and just like that, her transformation into dance/stage mum is complete.* HANNAH, *wrapped up in* UMMA's *unexpected joy, lets herself be carried by it—for now.*

HANNAH: Do you really think I could win?

UMMA: [*bad New York accent*] Stick with me kid, I make you a famous. Star … baby!

HANNAH: [*catching her reflection*] You know what? I like K-Hannah. Let me take you to dinner.

UMMA: No.

HANNAH: We can have a girls' night out.

UMMA: [*deep understanding*] Oh … Hannah wants to go to New York.

HANNAH: What?

UMMA: But first … We make them shit their leotards. Ready to jazz all that? Aud-ish-on video. ACTION!

> UMMA *turns on the disco lights. The introduction to the music starts.* UMMA *hits record.*

SCENE SIX

UMMA *has just finished a sale. The till is open, almost empty. She's sorting the last few coins when she notices something—the customer has forgotten his banana milk. She grabs it and hurries after him.*

UMMA: 아저씨! 잠깐만요! 우유 두고 가셨어요! *Ajeossi! jamkkanmanyo! uyu dugo gasyeosseoyo!* (Excuse me, sir! Sir, come back! You forgot your milk!)

> *She disappears outside.* HANNAH *enters, dressed in her tweed matching set, balancing boxes of fresh produce.* UMMA *returns.*

HANNAH: Feels like it's going to storm. The market was so busy. Something wrong? [*Pre-empting*] Oh no, did they call while I was out?

UMMA: No. Customer forgot his milk. Did she have gam?

HANNAH: Yep, they had persimmons.

UMMA: Put them next to gnome.

> HANNAH *plonks the boxes on the counter.*

HANNAH: I think they should have called by now.

UMMA: Email said they call by five p.m. It's only …

> *She looks at her phone.*

Oh … ten to five. So much time left. Just wait.

HANNAH: They're not calling. I didn't get on *Star Power*!

UMMA: You don't know—

HANNAH: [*stressed*] I should have done 'All That Jazz'.

UMMA: Hannah. K-pop-RAP-Nutbush was very … unique. I think they will call. Come on. Turn that frown the other way around.

HANNAH: I didn't want to let you down.

UMMA: When I worry too much … I get a Cosmopolitan.

HANNAH: What?

UMMA: I take you to concrete jungle where dreams are made of. Start spreading news. We leave today!

She grabs the television remote and pushes HANNAH *out of the mart. They disappear. For a moment, the mart sits empty.* UMMA's *arm pokes into the mart first, hitting play on the remote. The opening from* Sex and the City *plays. Then, with sudden theatricality,* UMMA *and* HANNAH *make a grand re-entrance.*

Welcome to big apple!

She puts her arm out to protect HANNAH.

Watch out for the cab.

Without hesitation, UMMA *marches straight up to the golden maneki-neko cat on the counter and begins speaking to it, as if it's a door attendant.*

[*To the maneki-neko*] I couldn't help but wonder … if you have a table for two? Yes? Thank you.

She puts her phone on top of the boxes and lifts them, struggling with the weight.

Aigo!

HANNAH: [*reaching to take it from her*] Here. Let me help.

UMMA *lets* HANNAH *help, then gestures to the counter.*

UMMA: Sit, sit down. You want beer? Soju?

They sit on opposite sides of the counter, like a bar.

[*Carrie Bradshaw impression, to a gnome*] 'I'd like a cheeseburger, please, large fries, and a Cosmopolitan.'

HANNAH: Have you been drinking while I was out?

UMMA *grabs soju from the fridge.*

UMMA: Hannah, when I … feel too much worry, I go to New York.

UMMA *gestures to the TV.*

I bingey watch. This is how I make my English so good … for you.

HANNAH: You've been practising for me?

Beat.

I tried to learn Korean—

UMMA nods, glances up at the TV.

UMMA: Oh … Oh …

Finally up to the bit she's been waiting for, UMMA *speaks in sync with the TV, as Carrie Bradshaw.*

'I couldn't help but wonder, are we all in search of something we can't have?'

She laughs.

HANNAH: You know all the lines off by heart.

UMMA: You are like Carrie. You never shut up.

HANNAH: Well, you are Mr. Big!

UMMA: Aigo!

HANNAH: Emotionally unavailable. Don't like change …

She cuts herself off, worried she's overstepped. UMMA *looks stern.*

UMMA: Shit! I am Mr. Big! … MEN! What for, eh? Always so … fake news. I don't need no man. You don't need no Sydney boyfriend.

HANNAH: It wasn't like that. He didn't do anything bad.

UMMA: I know why you came here so you can forget him. Get me soju glasses.

HANNAH: What? That's not why I'm here!

HANNAH *grabs some soju glasses off a shelf.*

UMMA: Shh … Forget I say, okay? Girls night out. Soju will fix. Korean way. Two hands. Never pour for yourself. Always turn from elders.

HANNAH: On my eighteenth birthday, I did a 'shoey'.

UMMA: What is shoey?

HANNAH: In Australia, on special occasions, we drink champagne from our shoes.

UMMA: 건배! *Geonbae!* (Cheers!)

HANNAH: 건배! *Geonbae!* We say *cheers.*

They clink soju glasses.

UMMA: Cheers!

HANNAH: Geonbae!

They drink. UMMA *presses* HANNAH*'s head to the side to remind her of the manners.*

UMMA: Now you pour for me.

HANNAH *pours the next round of soju.*

HANNAH: What if a customer comes in?

UMMA: I've served customers drunk before. 건배. *Geonbae.* (Cheers.)

HANNAH: 건배. *Geonbae.* (Cheers.) It doesn't even taste that alcoholic.

UMMA: Soju is …

She acts sneaky.

One minute you okay … next minute you lose your brain.

HANNAH: You're such a drama queen.

UMMA: [*proudly*] Koreans are the Italians of Asia. Oh, your pink goes cheeks, no more soju for you.

HANNAH: Mate. I grew up in Newcastle. I know how to drink. Hit me.

They both smash another shot.

UMMA: More?

HANNAH *puts forward her glass.*

Wah! Go Newcastle!

With each round of soju, they drink more, laugh more, and let their guards down—the bottle empties quickly.

HANNAH: Before I lose my brain, the lady at the market said something about the bill last week. She thought you were sick because you always pay on time.

UMMA: I fix.

HANNAH: She was a bit confused by me.

UMMA: You say you do summer job? You overseas student?

HANNAH: No I told her I'm your biological daughter.

UMMA: AIGO!!!

HANNAH: Just joking!

UMMA *pours another shot of soju for herself and drinks it.*

UMMA: I know her for many years. She would have been … very shocked.

HANNAH: Have you told anyone about me?

UMMA: [*suddenly*] Where I put my phone?

They look for UMMA'*s Samsung Galaxy.* UMMA *finds it in the box of persimmons.*

HANNAH: Did they call?

UMMA: Not yet.

HANNAH: They're not going to. We should just get back to work. I'll unpack the persimmons.

UMMA: Sit. Drink. I do later.

HANNAH: When did you last have time off?

UMMA *pauses, thinking.*

UMMA: When you came to Seoul last year. When we meet. I stop working that weekend … First time since my umma die.

HANNAH: What was it like for you?

UMMA: Hard. I don't like not working … makes day feel too long.

HANNAH: No, when we met.

UMMA: Oh—that was harder.

Beat.

HANNAH: Maybe you need someone here to help you out?

UMMA: Like you?

They both hesitate, uncertain if this is an invitation. The doorbell to the mart DING-DONGS.

HANNAH: Oh my god, it's a customer.

UMMA: I fix. [*Yelling at the door*] 마트 닫았어요! *Mateu dadasseoyo!*
[*In English*] MART IS CLOSED! BYYYYYEEEEE!
[*Serious*] I'm not drunk.

HANNAH: Noooooo. We're totally fine.

They both grip the counter to steady themselves.

UMMA: What is Newcastle like?

HANNAH: Kind of like Busan. Beach—

UMMA: Fish?

HANNAH: Ah, I'd say it's less known for its fish, more known for its bogans.

They both attempt to watch the TV, but the soju has settled in. Their bodies lean at odd angles, subtly swaying—each pretending not to notice how drunk the other has become. The fridge begins to smoke and flicker again. They both rise, in sync, wobbling slightly. Without a word, each move to either side of the fridge. They slap it—bam!—in perfect unison. The smoke stops. They exchange a look—relieved, maybe even proud.

If I win *Star Power*, I'll buy you a new fridge.

UMMA: I don't want. Still works. You can get me … K-pop.

HANNAH: Like concert tickets?

UMMA: K-pop … anything … everything. See, soju glasses are K-pop. I like stuff.

HANNAH: Yeah, I can see that.

UMMA: We don't have much when I was small, but we didn't need. But now, I think, maybe it's okay to have something for me … If I could buy as much K-pop as Carrie has shoes …

HANNAH: Why do you like *Sex and the City* so much?

Beat.

UMMA: Because the women are free … In this episode, Miranda move to Brooklyn so her son can have more room. I wish I go to America.

HANNAH: You can still go.

UMMA: When my umma was … not dead. I tell her I want to move but she say no.

HANNAH: Didn't she want you to be happy?

UMMA: Happy is hard when you are poor. She was born during the Korean War … she only know a hard life. She made this mart from nothing.

HANNAH: What would you do if you weren't working here?

UMMA: That is a stupid question.

HANNAH: No, it's not.

UMMA: Okay. Fine. I'd go on *Star Power*, become famous singer. Win money. Retire to Manhattan. Have ten cats.

HANNAH: That sounds amazing.

UMMA: Too late. I have the mart. I have gnomes. I'm not a turtle.

She demonstrates with Turtle Chips, moves to different shelf.

I can't just move my home. They say the air is clean in Australia. You have more room there than life in Korea. More … happy for you.

HANNAH: But why couldn't I have been happy growing up in Korea?

UMMA: You had bad life?

HANNAH: I'm not here because my life is bad.

UMMA: Why you here Hannah?

HANNAH: Because I've missed you.

> *Beat.*

Umma. That's Mummy in Korean, right?

UMMA: Yes.

HANNAH: Can I call you Umma?

> UMMA*'s phone rings. The* Sex and the City *theme plays as her ringtone. Thunder cracks.* UMMA *answers just as the final note fades.*

UMMA: [*to phone*] 여보세요. *Yeoboseyo.* (Hello.)

> *The storm has arrived. The lightbulb flickers above, casting an unsteady shadow between them.*

[*To phone*] 네 … 네. *Ne … Ne.* (Yes … yes.)

> *Beat.*

네 … 감사합니다. *Ne. Gamsahamnida.* (Yes … thank you.)

> *She hangs up.*

[*To* HANNAH] We have to get back to work.

> HANNAH*'s face doesn't match* UMMA*'s excitement. The fridge lightbulb sputters, then goes out. Darkness descends on the mart.*

SCENE SEVEN

The drumbeats of a famous K-pop song[8] shake the mart. The golden maneki-neko waves in sync with the music. The garden gnomes have migrated again. Three now sit behind the counter like judges. Three swing display stands have been spread out like studio cameras, labelled '1', '2', '3' with numbers scrawled on scrap cardboard.

Offstage, UMMA *yells.*

UMMA: Camera Two!

> UMMA *wheels* HANNAH *in on a trolley.* HANNAH *poses dramatically to Camera Two (swing stand).*

---

8. The lyric placement is a guide, invented for the script. In production, it should reflect the K-pop song chosen for the *Star Power* performance in Scene Nine, as determined by each production.

HANNAH: My love is like—boom cha, boom cha cha
My heart goes boom cha cha

UMMA *slaps the remote. The karaoke machine cuts the music.*

UMMA: Go again. From the top.
HANNAH: [*panting*] Can we have a break?
UMMA: K-pop idols train for years. You only have one week.
HANNAH: That's why I think I should just do 'All That Jazz'.
UMMA: AISH! This is *Star Power*. You do K-pop. I know best.
HANNAH: Do I have to do the whole chorus to Camera Two?
UMMA: I told you, do boom cha cha to judges!

UMMA *points at the gnomes. Their painted expressions remain unchanged, but somehow, it feels as though their eyes are rolling in silent judgment.*

HANNAH: I can't concentrate when I'm hungry.
UMMA: You want to win, you do what I say. ACTION!

UMMA *takes* HANNAH *for another spin in the trolley.* HANNAH *sings without the backing track.*

HANNAH: Love me like—boom cha, boom cha cha. Boom boom cha cha cha.
UMMA: You look like potato going for a ride. Stick bum out more.

HANNAH *'s bum sticks out awkwardly as she clings to the trolley.*

HANNAH: [*offbeat, struggling*] No more lies—boom cha cha—
[*To gnomes*] No goodbyes—boom cha cha
UMMA: [*yelling at* HANNAH *'s posture*] BUM! BUM!
HANNAH: Am I doing it?
UMMA: No! You need to look like sexy Asian baby girl, not poo!

She demonstrates a sultry bend.

Do it like me? Oppa, are you spicy like gochujang?
HANNAH: I need a break. I'm starving.
UMMA: Have watermelon.
HANNAH: All I've eaten today is watermelon. I want ramyun.
UMMA: You on K-pop diet. Famous singer. He only eat tofu and run six hours every day so he look right way.
HANNAH: I'm not a real K-pop star.

UMMA: How much you weigh?

HANNAH: I dunno … around sixty kilos?

UMMA: WAH! Korean girls can't be more than fifty kilos.

HANNAH: I can't lose ten kilos in one week!

UMMA: Watermelon only.

HANNAH: In Australia, I'm normal.

UMMA: In Korea, you are extra-extra-large.

HANNAH: You know what, this isn't fun anymore!

    HANNAH *storms off towards the apartment.*

UMMA: When things are not fun, you don't run away. If it's hard, you have to keep going. You work. My umma taught me that!

HANNAH: Well, I don't have my umma!

    Beat.

UMMA: I can't take a day off work. I can't take you to climb Namsan Mountain. I can't give you good life. But if you win *Star Power* …

HANNAH: So, this is about the prize money?

UMMA: If you win, you can have all the things I can't give you. I fix. I make you happy.

HANNAH: I am happy. Just hanging out with you.

    Beat.

You're right. It's better if I do the whole chorus to Camera Two.

UMMA: Okay. You finish looking at Camera Three gnome. ACTION!

    She turns on the music. HANNAH *hits her choreography with power and precision—body sharp, eyes sad but determined, dancing through everything they cannot say.* UMMA *leads her into the song.*

UMMA: My love is like—boom cha, boom cha cha
    My heart goes boom cha cha

HANNAH: [*shouts*] GNOMES!

HANNAH/UMMA: Love me like—boom cha, boom cha cha
    Boom boom cha cha cha

SCENE EIGHT

In a blink, the mart vanishes, replaced by the glitz and glamour of Star Power. *But* UMMA *and* HANNAH *don't quite match its sparkle yet. They are suspended in the transition, caught between two worlds—one they know and one they are just beginning to step into.* UMMA *and* HANNAH *can only just be seen through clouds of hairspray and make-up. A competitor can be heard singing in the background.*

HANNAH: I've done three poos.

UMMA: You look too small to hold that much poo.

> UMMA *adjusts* HANNAH*'s K-girl outfit.*

HANNAH: Leave it, it's fine.

UMMA: You are on last. I go check where they are up to. Warm up.

> UMMA *exits.* HANNAH *stands alone, the audience's applause swells, a tide replacing the storm outside. She had never been to South Korea in summer—typhoon season. Hardly the best time to be a tourist. Hardly the best time to come back.*
>
> HANNAH *practises her dance nervously, tugging at her skirt, willing it to stretch lower.* UMMA *enters. She watches as* HANNAH *rehearses. She yells at* HANNAH *from the wings.*

UMMA: No!

HANNAH: I know! I made a mistake. It's trolley, rap. Tap.

UMMA: Camera Three. Turn. Gnomes—I mean, judges.

HANNAH: Oh god, I'm too nervous, let's just leave now while no one else is here.

> UMMA *reaches out to* HANNAH, *her hand soft but firm as she taps her gently on the back. For the first time since* HANNAH*'s arrival, they truly look at each other.* UMMA *retrieves something from her bag. It's a blue apron, folded so the audience can't see the front.*

UMMA: I have something for you. This was my umma's. Your grandmother. Your Halmeoni. In Hollywood movies, they say, '*She would want you to have it.*' But why she want to give her granddaughter an old shit apron? So … I fix!

She reveals the full blue apron.

I *'vajazzle'* the front just like Charlotte did in *Sex and the City*.

HANNAH: I think she added bling to a different front.

UMMA *puts on her orange apron. A gold 'K' and 'STAR' motif twinkles among the constellation of bling.*

UMMA: I vajazzle mine too! So, we can be matching.

HANNAH: I don't want to ruin this generational pass down of bling apron moment, but I'm literally shitting myself.

UMMA: Oh—shit.

HANNAH: I've got to go do poo number four.

UMMA: Hannah! There's no more poo. You will be okay.

HANNAH *nervously paces around.*

HANNAH: Why the fuck am I tap-dancing on a random Korean television show?!

UMMA: It's okay. We can fix this. What did you do when you were pooing yourself before eis-tedd-fods?

HANNAH: I dunno, I was twelve! Mum and Dad would give me a pep talk—

UMMA: You go, girl!

HANNAH: And a hug.

UMMA: Okay … Just pretend this is just eis-tedd—

HANNAH: I was tap-dancing at the Newcastle Town Hall, not on LIVE TV in Seoul in front of millions of people.

UMMA: Okay. Okay. This is bad, we need big fix. We ask my umma for help. It's been a while, but we can give it a trial.

UMMA *kneels in prayer.*

HANNAH: Wait. Are we religious?

UMMA: Sometimes. When needed. You need to bow too.

HANNAH *gets on the ground.*

엄마 … 축복해 주세요. *Umma … chukbokhae juseyo.* (Mother, we ask you for your blessing.)

Hannah. Now you go. ACTION!

HANNAH: Grandmother. Halmeoni. I … I um … Hello … Anneyong …

She pulls out her iPhone to use her translation app.

I can't do it in Korean.

UMMA: Ancestors don't need translation app.

HANNAH: Halmeoni, please … What are we praying for?

UMMA: [*in prayer*] Ancestors, we want to win *Star Power*. Help Hannah dance good.

HANNAH: And … sing … good.

UMMA: Some of the notes are very high. [*To* HANNAH] When you want something big, you don't go alone. You go with all your family behind you, even the ones you can't see.

HANNAH: Should I pray to my dad?

UMMA: [*sharply*] No!

HANNAH: I think we need as many family members as possible. Father … Appa?

UMMA: Stop. No Appa!

A male voice, the floor manager of Star Power *calls from offstage.*

VOICE: 광고 끝나고 바로 무대에 올라가야 해요. 백스테이지로 와주세요. *Gwanggo kkeutnago baro mudae-e ollagaya haeyo. Baekseuteiji-ro wajuseyo.* (You are on after the commercial break. Please come backstage.)

UMMA: You on when commercial finish.

HANNAH: Why can't I pray to him?

UMMA: He won't be there for us.

HANNAH: He's my dad.

UMMA: We no praying to him.

HANNAH: Why don't you like him?

UMMA: In Korea, we don't speak bad of the dead. Let's go!

UMMA goes and realises HANNAH *isn't following.*

What are you doing?

HANNAH starts trying take off her outfit, but she can't untie her apron.

Without good K-look you won't win.

FLOOR MANAGER: [*voiceover*] 준비하세요. 곧 당신의 공연 시간이에요. *Junbihaseyo. Got dangsinui gongyeon sigani-eyo.* (Please get ready. It's nearly your time to perform.)

UMMA: You're on next. Stop. You don't get the Korean way.

HANNAH: I'm trying. I've done everything you wanted … the clothes … bit I still don't feel Korean.

UMMA: What do you want from me?

HANNAH: I need to know who I am. Tell me about my father.

UMMA: He left me.

VOICE: 준비하세요. 곧 다음 참가자 공연 시간이에요. *Junbihaseyo. Got daeum chamgaja gongyeon sigani-eyo.* (Please get ready. It's nearly your time to perform.)

HANNAH: Why … why didn't you tell me?

VOICE: 열 *yeol* (ten) … 아홉 *ahop* (nine) … 여덟 *yeodeol* (eight) …

UMMA: I try and let him stay a good dream for you.

> UMMA *pushes* HANNAH *onto the stage, then retreats to the side of the stage.*

VOICE: 일곱 *ilgop* (seven) … 여섯 *yeoseot* (six) …

HANNAH: I need to know.

VOICE: 다섯 *daseot* (five) … 넷 *net* (four) …

UMMA: Not now.

VOICE: 셋 *set* (three) … 둘 *dul* (two) … 하나 *hana* (one) …

UMMA: You're on! ACTION!

> *The lights dim, and the introduction to the K-pop song plays.* HANNAH *runs into position. Lights swirl over the studio audience as their cheers grow louder. The announcement booms in Korean and English, with US accent.*

VOICE: [*host*] 호주 시드니에서 가장 큰 K 환영 인사를 보내주세요. 한나!!! *Hoju Sideunieseo gajang keun K hwan-yeong insaleul bonaejuseyo. Hannah!!!* (Please give your biggest K-welcome to HANNAH!!!)

> *The audience cheers.* HANNAH *nervously delivers her introduction.*

HANNAH: G'day mate! I'm Hannah—born in Korea, raised in Australia. Adopted as a baby, now reunited with my umma.
By day, I stack shelves in her mart. By night?

> *She fumbles.*

She dreams …

> *She glances to* UMMA—*who gives the thumbs up.*

I dream of being a singer.
I've got heart. I've got moves … But—do I have *Star Power*?

She hits her opening pose. The music crashes in. HANNAH *forces a smile. The beat drops.*

[*Singing*] My love is like—boom cha, boom cha cha
My heart goes boom cha cha
Love me like—boom cha, boom cha cha

She falters.

Boom boom cha cha cha

UMMA: [*from side stage*] Gnome … I mean Camera Two.

HANNAH: No more lies—boom cha cha
No goodbyes—boom cha cha

She tries to keep going.

This is mine—boom cha cha

She starts faltering.

My heart goes boom cha cha …

She stops singing but the music keeps playing. HANNAH *starts spiralling.*

UMMA: Hannah. Keep going. Five, six … five, six, seven—

HANNAH: You don't want to be seen with me in the mart, but you're okay with me being on national television?

UMMA: Why would you want to be seen with me after what I did?

The microphones emit a sharp squeal, abruptly cutting off the music.

I don't want to embar … embarr …

HANNAH: You don't embarrass me. I'm not embarrassed by who I am.

VOICE: [*host*] 무대를 떠나 주세요. *Mudae-reul tteona juseyo.* (Please leave the stage.)

HANNAH: Whatever we do, whatever we try … it's never enough. Even if we win this … it won't *fix* anything.

UMMA: No no no … I fix. I fix!

HANNAH: [*looking at cameras*] Are they still filming?

UMMA: We work hard. Keeping going.

UMMA *steps onto the stage.*

HANNAH: I can't—

UMMA: Hannah … remember? I sing 'Arirang'. / It's about—
HANNAH: I want to / go.
UMMA: Crossing / mountain—
HANNAH: I want to go home.
UMMA: Hannah! I fix!

> UMMA *steps into the centre of the stage, bathed in the spotlight. The song pours out of her, powerful and unrestrained, as if this moment was her destiny—to be a star, to become the singer, the woman she was always meant to be.* UMMA*'s voice is not perfect. It is not polished. But it is true. And that truth is enough. For the first time in her life, she is seen. Truly free.* HANNAH *watches.*

아리랑, 아리랑, 아라리요 … 아리랑 고개로 넘어간다. *Arirang, Arirang, arariyo … Arirang gogaero neomeoganda.* (Arirang, Arirang, oh, Arirang, crossing the Arirang Pass.)

나를 버리고 가시는 님은. 십리도 못가서 발병난다. *Nareul beorigo gasineun nimeun. Siprido motgaseo balbyeongnanda.* (The one who abandons me won't make it ten miles without falling ill.)

청천하늘엔 잔별도 많고. 우리네 가슴엔 희망도 많다. *Cheongcheon haneuren janbyeoldo manko. Urine gaseumeun huimangdo manta.* (There are countless stars in the blue sky. And there is much hope in our hearts.)

저기 저 산이 백두산이라지. 동지 섣달에도 꽃만 핀다. *Jeogi jeo sani Baekdusan iraji. Dongji seotdaledo kkonman pinda.* (That mountain there, Baekdusan, blooms even in the dead of winter.)

저기 저 산이 백두산이라지. 동지 섣달에도 꽃만 핀다. *Jeogi jeo sani Baekdusan iraji. Dongji seotdaledo kkonman pinda.* (That mountain there, Baekdusan, blooms even in the dead of winter.)

> HANNAH *steps back, bowing slightly—not to the audience, but to* UMMA. *And then, quietly, she disappears into the wings.*

SCENE NINE

The mart door creaks open. The lights are too bright against the dark outside. UMMA *enters first, clutching the* Star Power *trophy. She sets it down without ceremony, like it's another item to be shelved. She starts refilling ramyun cups like it's any other night. She moves slowly, mechanically, trying to will the night back into something normal.* HANNAH, *changed back into her usual clothes, hesitates in the doorway, the night air still clinging to her.*

UMMA: You hungry?

> HANNAH *sets her bag down. Watches* UMMA.

I make ramyun.

> *She moves automatically to the food station.* HANNAH *lingers near the door.*

HANNAH: You're acting like nothing happened.

UMMA: No customer come this late. Good time to clean mart.

> *She busies herself, straightening chip packets, brushing invisible dust.*

HANNAH: You really think we can just … go back to normal?

UMMA: Work is the only thing that stays.

HANNAH: I'm still here. Tell me about him.

UMMA: Can we do this tomorrow?

HANNAH: I won't be here.

UMMA: You leaving?

HANNAH: Yes. And I don't think I'll come back.

> *Beat.*

UMMA: We met at school. He know, after class, I work at mart. Every day. In the summer, he bring me gam. Persimmon. My favourite. After school, the boys go to military service. Before he leave, he promise me, when he come back, we will marry. I believe him because he never miss a day of fruit. I wait for him. I think I feel sick because I miss him too much.

HANNAH: What happened when you told him you were pregnant?

UMMA: I don't know where he was. I don't know where to write. No phone in mart back then.

HANNAH: So, he never knew about me?

UMMA: No. Every day I pray he come back. I hide you under apron, but you grow bigger. My umma, she was dis—disa—

HANNAH: Disappointed.

UMMA: In mart, people whisper, they ask questions. If customers find out, I'm not married, and I have baby, I bring shame to my family. They won't shop at mart. My umma make me go away. Home for unwed mothers. I push all night. I hear you cry. I see your pink feet when they take you away. They tell us—never think about baby again. Baby will have real mother, happy life. I didn't want to come back here. But how would he know where to find me?

HANNAH: My father ... he promised you ... he would come back, but he didn't?

UMMA: No. I wait for him, so many summers. Then I find out. After military, he move to America. But there was accident. He was too young. I thought you both gone forever.

> *Beat.*

HANNAH: Every year on my birthday, I thought of you. Did you think about me too?

> *Beat.*

I dreamed about him, but ... I wished for you.

UMMA: You had good life?

HANNAH: Yes. I had a good life. But ... I felt guilty. Like missing you meant I was ungrateful. I mean ... how can you miss someone you've never met? But isn't normal? Isn't it only human? To miss my mother?

UMMA: How am I your mother?

HANNAH: You gave me life.

UMMA: You think that's enough?

HANNAH: When we met, I thought I'd feel like I was coming home. But when you hugged me ... I felt like I was drowning.

UMMA: They didn't let me hold you when you were born. Maybe that's why I don't know how to hold you.

HANNAH: Then let me hold you.

UMMA: I can't.

HANNAH: Why do you make everything so hard?

UMMA: Why does everything have to be the way you want it?

HANNAH: Because it was me who found us. Me—doing the paperwork, saving the money here. I'm the reason we're standing here. Was it better when you didn't know me?

UMMA: You spend all your life trying to remember me, and I spend all of mine trying to forget. I need time.

HANNAH: I couldn't wait any longer. I wanted …

UMMA: Want, want, want. More, more, more. I gave you everything. You go to school. You go to university.

HANNAH: You think an education, a career will make up for losing you, Umma?

UMMA: Why you keep calling me that?

HANNAH: You never answer me.

UMMA: 나도 힘들어. 편하게 말하고 싶은데, 안 돼. *Nado himdeureo. Pyeonhage malhago sip-eunde, an dwae.* [*Then, in English, struggling*] I think in Korean. But I have to speak to you in English. I'm tired … I wish we could speak free …

HANNAH: I've tried to learn Korean. But the words … they don't fit in my mouth. No matter how many times I repeat them. No matter how many times I hear them. The words will never be mine.

    Beat.

UMMA: I like cats, dogs too loud. Pink my favourite colour. Red beans bad.

HANNAH: What?

UMMA: You get here and ask so many questions, but you don't wait for answers. I think of you, Hannah. Every birthday. Every night before I sleep. You think I forget my own baby?

HANNAH: I don't know how to stop wanting all the things we never had.

UMMA: When you lose things—you can't go back and get them again. You have good life. Like Carrie. Miranda. Samantha. Charlotte?

HANNAH: Yes. But I still needed you.

UMMA: My umma was hard. She never forgive me. After you born, I came back to her but she never look at me with soft eyes again.

I fail—so she fail, you see? Mummy's love can be too hard to understand. I want you free from that kind of love.

Beat.

HANNAH: My boyfriend wanted to have kids. But I didn't know if I wanted to. He waited so long for me—but it wasn't fair. So yeah … we broke up and I ran. How can I be a mum if I don't even know mine? I'm too Korean to be Australian, too Australian to be Korean. I don't want to have a baby who is stuck in the middle like me. How can I give a home to a child, when I'm still trying to find one myself?

Beat.

I think I came here because I didn't know who else to ask. Do you think I could be a mother?

UMMA: Perfect umma live in dreams. Not in real life. No one gets it right.

HANNAH: I'm scared I will be too … hard.

UMMA: Let go of being perfect mum. I can't be that, and neither can you.

HANNAH: You can't be my umma?

UMMA: I try … but it doesn't fit. I make this way a long time ago.

HANNAH: No, you can. I'm here now. Try holding me again?

> HANNAH *stretches out her arms—starts drowning again.* UMMA *doesn't move.*

UMMA: You need to learn to live with hurt. Hannah, this hurt—is part of who you are.

Beat.

HANNAH: I'd never seen anyone who looked like me. Not a single photo, nothing. It took me so many years to find you. Coming to Korea, meeting you, knowing you were actually *real*, made me so happy. But when I went back to Sydney, I felt even more lost than before. I saw parts of you in my face—but not enough to make it whole. We've lost so many years together. So many hugs.

UMMA: Your appa … I remember him standing just like that. He think so deep—like you. And I would remind him, come back. Come back to *now*.

HANNAH: Do you think he would've liked me?

UMMA: Yes. You have his eyes.

HANNAH: I do?

UMMA: Sometimes … it's hard for me to see. But yes. You do.

HANNAH: Did you want to keep me?

UMMA: I can't fix what's lost. But maybe … we can start again.

HANNAH: Are you sure you can't be my mother?

UMMA: We can be what we are now. Call me Soon Hee. That's who I am.

SCENE TEN

A young woman enters holding a persimmon.

GAM: The Autumn Harvest celebration, Chuseok, has come and gone. A young man in a crisp military uniform enters the mart. He carries a small tray of vivid, ripe persimmons. 'Soon Hee? Soon Hee?' No one comes. He places the tray on the counter and picks up a piece of paper.

A woman in a blue apron enters. She watches him as he writes.

He hears something and looks up. '*Soon Hee?*' But it's not Soon Hee. It's her mother.

'*My daughter doesn't work here anymore. She's gone.*'

'*Halmeoni, could you please tell me where she is?*' She shakes her head.

'*Please leave now. You're disrupting my work.*'

'*Please, Halmeoni. I need to speak with her.*'

'*Get out of my shop. Get out now.*'

The young man understands when elders feel disrespected, there are no further avenues for resolution. With a humble bow, he takes his leave.

'*I will let you get back to work.*' He says. '*Goodbye.*'

Halmeoni picks up the note. The room seems to blur. Her heart swells into her throat. Her lips part to call out to him—but no sound comes. Memories flood back, as if her daughter is standing right in front of her, confessing her love for the boy. She picks up a perfect persimmon. It feels cool against her warm, trembling palm.

She takes out the orange apron from below the counter, cradling it like the granddaughter she will never get to hold. Her daughter would have had the baby now. She should have already returned home.

She did what any mother would do. What she thought was best for her daughter.

The boy enters again. Determined not to give up on his love. He watches as Halmeoni scrunches the note in her fist. He has the answer he needs. As he walks away, he seems a little heavier than when he first entered. Each step takes him further from Soon Hee and promises of yesterday. He will never return.

SCENE ELEVEN

SOON HEE *enters with a tray of persimmon. They sit on the counter as the mart undergoes a vibrant transformation. Bright posters of K-pop bands adorn the walls.* HANNAH *and* SOON HEE *carry and place down a celebratory flower stand. It stands proudly by the door beneath a 'GRAND REOPENING' banner.* HANNAH *sees the gnomes grouped together like a family next to the persimmons.*

SOON HEE: Gnomes look good all together, don't you think?

HANNAH: There's a line around the block.

SOON HEE: Everyone wants to come to meet the famous TV stars. Now we have a K-pop mart. I think we should give it a new name.

HANNAH: What were you thinking?

SOON HEE: We make it more Korean.

HANNAH: By adding a K?

SOON HEE: Welcome to … K-mart!!!

HANNAH: A very *unique* name for a shop. I thought I would only be here for the summer.

SOON HEE: But the autumn trees look much prettier, eh?

HANNAH: You're happy I'm staying a little longer?

SOON HEE: Okay.

HANNAH: I need you to give me a bit more than that.

SOON HEE: I am enjoying … hanging out.

HANNAH: I came here to get to know *you*, but, I feel like I know *me* more now.

SOON HEE: [*US accent*] 'The most exciting, challenging, and significant relationship of all is the one you have with yourself.'

HANNAH: Carrie Bradshaw?

SOON HEE: She is annoying … but wise.

HANNAH: Are we ready to open?

> HANNAH *walks towards the door.*

SOON HEE: Hannah. I'm sorry.

HANNAH: I'm sorry too.

SOON HEE: I am very sorry.

HANNAH: You know I never meant to hurt you?

SOON HEE: I know. Me too.

HANNAH: I just couldn't live with myself if I didn't try and find you.

SOON HEE: I'm happy you did. I am like a mountain. I was always waiting. You are ocean. Always moving.

HANNAH: Do you think this was always how it was meant to be?

SOON HEE: In Korea, the mountains are never far from the sea.

HANNAH: If we lose each other again—I'll wait for you.

SOON HEE: You promise?

HANNAH: Yes. We have time. And we can return to each other, where the mountains meet the sea.

> *Beat.*

Everyone thinks finding each other is the happy ending. But no one tells you how to live afterwards. Soon Hee, I want to be your friend.

UMMA: Me too Hannah.

HANNAH: What do you see when you look at me?

SOON HEE: My friend.

HANNAH: You're nothing like what I imagined.

SOON HEE: I'm too fabulous to be imagined.

HANNAH: Is that from *Sex and the City*?

SOON HEE: No. Me. Soon Hee.

HANNAH: Soon Hee. Are you happy I'm here?

SOON HEE: Not happy. No. How do you say?

> SOON HEE *grabs the remote and presses some buttons.*

[*Speaking*] Take my hand—Hannah, you are my euphoria.

> *She hits play on the remote and sings the lyrics of the chorus with the music.*

You are the cause of my euphoria.

BTS's 'Euphoria' plays through the mart. The song continues to play as they finish preparing the mart for opening. Their partnership, a quiet, modern take on the Nongbu[9] tradition— shared labour, shared care, building something fragile but real. They move around each other, stacking boxes, adjusting gnomes. Small, ordinary tasks. The slow, daily work of building a life with someone you barely know.

SOON HEE *stops the music. For a moment, neither moves. Then— almost shyly—*SOON HEE *opens her arms.* HANNAH *steps into them. They hug. Then, together, they open the door, embarking on a journey full of unknown possibilities.*

THE END

---

9. 농부 NONGBU women carried the weight of the fields and the family on their backs. They were the quiet endurance behind every harvest, the unseen strength that held generations together—working, surviving, expecting nothing, giving everything. Through wars, colonisation, and poverty, they kept the country alive when everything else was falling apart.

GRIFFIN THEATRE COMPANY PRESENTS
IN ASSOCIATION WITH BELVOIR ST THEATRE

KOREABOO

BY MICHELLE LIM DAVIDSON

4 JUN – 20 JUL 2025
DOWNSTAIRS THEATRE, BELVOIR ST THEATRE

GRIFFIN
THEATRE
COMPANY

CAST & CREATIVES

Director Jessica Arthur
Dramaturg Julian Larnach
Designer Mel Page
Lighting Designer Kate Baldwin
Composer & Sound Designer Brendon Boney
Community Engagement Lead Korean Adoptees in Australia Network (KAIAN)
Design Associate James Stibilj
Development Associate Andrew Undi Lee
Production Manager Sherydan Simson
Stage Manager Jen Jackson

With Michelle Lim Davidson, Heather Jeong

SPECIAL THANKS

Charles An (Voiceover work), Lauryn Bae Brokate, Korea Liquor, Shaun Kwak,
Renee Lim, Oriental Merchant, Candy Park, Lauren Proietti, Angela Nica Sullen
(Acting/Voice Coach), Cassandra Sorrell, Brigid Zengeni, JoJo Zhou.

PRESENTING PARTNER

BELVOIR ST THEATRE

SUPPORTED BY

GRIFFIN STUDIO WORKSHOP

MALCOLM ROBERTSON FOUNDATION

GOVERNMENT PARTNERS

Australian Government

Creative Australia

NSW GOVERNMENT

Koreaboo was developed as part of Griffin Studio, an initiative of Griffin
Theatre Company, with support from the Malcolm Robertson Foundation
and Griffin Studio donors, and the Griffin Redraft Fund.

PLAYWRIGHT'S NOTE

When I was growing up on Awabakal land, in a small suburb of Newcastle, there was no one who looked like me. I was often startled by my own reflection—expecting to see a blonde, blue-eyed beach kid, and instead seeing a dark-haired, brown-eyed girl staring back.

For a long time, I believed my adoption was an isolated event, a private twist of fate. But when I began searching for my biological family, I realised my story wasn't the exception. It was part of a much longer history, one that connects me to thousands of others.

Since the 1950s, over 200,000 Korean children have been sent abroad for adoption, raised across Europe, North America and Australia. Despite being the largest group of intercountry adoptees in Australia—more than 3,600 since the late 1960s—our stories have remained largely unexplored. For decades, adoption narratives were shaped by adoptive families, governments, and institutions—rarely in our own words. That is changing. Across the globe, a community of Korean adoptees is rising, reclaiming its past and redefining its future.

This play is one small part of that reclamation. It was inspired by my life, but it's not a documentary. It's imagined from reality. With the support of my families in both Australia and Korea, I've written it from the inside out.

In 2019, I was rehearsing a play at Griffin when I got a call from my social worker. After years of searching, my first correspondence from my birth family had arrived—letters, photos, faces.

In those images, I saw—a nose, lips and eyes shaped like mine. I thought it would bring clarity. Instead, it opened a quiet kind of confusion.

A history I'd only imagined was now real—but still distant. I couldn't quite see myself in it. It unsettled me—a change I didn't have words for yet.

I couldn't have predicted how my relationship with Korea, my family, or myself would evolve—or that something so private would become something to share. Something light, funny, even a little absurd.

Maybe Koreaboo began back then—and maybe it was always meant to find its way back to Griffin. Now, standing here with this play, I see myself clearly. Not as unfamiliar. But whole.

This story is deeply personal, but it wasn't created alone. It grew through collaboration. I'm deeply grateful to **Jess Arthur, Julian Larnach, Andrew 'Undi' Lee, Heather Jeong, Jen Jackson** and the creative team, for their heart and insight. And to those who joined us throughout development —thank you for your time and care.

Thank you to the Griffin Studio program and to **Declan** and everyone at Griffin for going above and beyond to support this story. This work wouldn't exist without the generous backing of donors and the Board. It's through this kind of collective support that new work can thrive.

Thank you to Belvoir, Shanahan Management, Cameron's Management, **Sally McClennan, Simon and Jessie Whipp, Jonah Klein, Polly Rowe, Lauryn Bae Brokate, Josh Price, Cameron Stead, Wade Jackson, Eloise Winestock, Michelle Law, Alex Papps, Vanessa Downing, Bradley Hall, Renee Billinghurst, Margaret Watson, Su Park**, my friends, family, and the Korean Adoptee community—your support made this possible.

PLAYWRIGHT'S NOTE

I'm fortunate to have reconnected with my Korean family. Every adoptee—if they wish—should have that chance. Reunion shouldn't depend on luck or personal resources. It should be supported, resourced and treated with care.

To ask where you come from, or to feel what you feel, shouldn't require permission. These are rights, not privileges. And yet, for many adoptees, those rights remain out of reach—denied by systems that have long prioritised secrecy over connection.

What's needed is lasting support—legal, emotional and cultural. True advocacy makes space for every stage. It asks us to meet those shaped by adoption with compassion and respect, not judgement. And to offer care that honours their experience, and the freedom to grow without carrying anyone else's expectations.

Reunion isn't always what we see in films. It can be awkward. Incomplete. It doesn't always bring answers, just different questions.

Koreaboo wasn't written to fix the past or offer tidy answers. It's an invitation into a story felt by many but seen by few, where hope and disappointment sit side by side. Where connection doesn't offer resolution, only the chance to begin.

It holds that attempt.
It asks questions out loud.
It stays with what doesn't resolve.
It doesn't offer a solution.
It offers relationship and an acknowledgment of the quiet courage it takes to keep showing up and learn how to love someone as they are.

Years ago, I went looking for someone who looked like me.

Now I offer this story back, hoping someone else might feel a little less alone.

**Michelle Lim Davidson 임현우
Playwright**

DIRECTOR'S NOTE

I was in a shop with **Michelle** when she spotted a pink cat keyboard. She very seriously decided that the keyboard would give legitimacy to her writing process. Michelle, of course, knew it was a seriously ridiculous statement; this is an encapsulation of what is unique about Michelle and her storytelling.

Her sense of fun is nuanced with a depth of empathy which clarifies life's confusions. Her lively inner world colours her expression of the ineffable—approaching others with compassion. Her silliness disarms, allowing humour to draw out confronting truths concerning how we relate to others.

Michelle is Korean; but she is also Australian and an adoptee. Her experience is one defined by thresholds of belonging. Her ability to shed dignity on the experiences of others, as well as a sensitivity to how she herself is perceived, lends the character of both Hannah and her birth mother a fullness and brightness—a clarity of sight and voice that deepens their shared experience.

Michelle asks, how do we move forward with respect for the past? She answers with kindness and an acknowledgement that in recognising the complexity of relationships—we can begin to heal.

We are invited to share in Michelle's generous insights into the difficulties and demands of love, identity and belonging—and given the space to unravel our own challenges with such things. Michelle has spent hundreds of hours enriching every line, crafting her unique story—all on a pink cat keyboard.

Thank you to **Heather**, **Julian** and **Undi** for their dedication to the work. Thanks to **Brendon**, **Kate**, **Mel**, **Jen**, **Sherydan**, **James**, **Candy** and **Angela** for their thoughtful contributions, and to Griffin and KAIAN for all their support.

Most of all, thanks to Michelle for sharing her perspective, story and culture so generously.

Jessica Arthur

BIOGRAPHIES

MICHELLE LIM DAVIDSON
PLAYWRIGHT / HANNAH

Michelle's theatre credits include: for Griffin Theatre Company: *The Lysicrates Prize* and *The Feather in the Web* for which she was nominated for Best Female Actress in a Mainstage Production at the Sydney Theatre Awards; for Melbourne Theatre Company: *A Streetcar Named Desire*, *Torch the Place*, *An Ideal Husband*; for Sydney Theatre Company: *On The Beach*, *Banging Denmark*, *How to Rule the World*, *Top Girls* and *Power Plays*; for Ensemble Theatre; *The Plant and Seminar*; and for ABC: *Play School Live*.

Michelle's television credits include for ABC: *The Newsreader* Seasons 1-3 for which she received a Logie and two AACTA nominations for Best Supporting Actress in a Television Drama, *Play School*, *Get Krack!n* and *Utopia* which received the Equity Award for Outstanding Performance by an Ensemble in a Comedy Series; for Channel 9: *After the Verdict* and *Doctor Doctor*; for Ten Network: *The Secrets She Keeps* and for BBC: *Top of the Lake: China Girl*.

Film credits include *Goldstone* and *Beyond the Bubble* selected for the Sydney Film Festival.

Michelle is a Commonwealth representative on the Board of the Australian Children's Television Foundation. As a screen writer, she has written for ABC Kids and ABC ME and serves as a script consultant on *The Newsreader*. Her play *Where We Love is Home* was shortlisted for the Patrick White Award. Michelle was a member of Griffin Theatre Company's 2023 Griffin Studio.

BIOGRAPHIES

JESSICA ARTHUR
DIRECTOR

Jessica Arthur is a theatre director celebrated for her storytelling through movement and commitment to new Australian work.

For Griffin Theatre Company: as Director: *The Martin Lysicrates Prize*.

Other theatre credits include, as Director: for Belvoir St Theatre: *Lose to Win*, *The Wolves*; for Kings Cross Theatre: *Two Hearts*; for La Mama Theatre: *Intoxication*; for National Institute of Dramatic Art: *Kindness, Realism, Rausch*; for Never Never Theatre Company: *Unend*; for Old Fitz Theatre: *All The Fraudulent Horse Girls*, *Lose to Win*; for Redline Productions: *The Bugalugs Bum Thief*; for State Theatre Company of South Australia and Sydney Theatre Company: *The Dictionary of Lost Words*, *Chalkface*; for Sydney Theatre Company: *The Tenant of Wildfell Hall*, *Grand Horizons*, *Home*, *I'm Darling*, *Wonnangatta*, *Banging Denmark*, *Mosquitoes*, *Lethal Indifference*; as Associate Director: *The Tempest*, *Julius Caesar*; as Assistant Director: *The Harp in the South Parts I & II*, *Dinner*, *Chimerica*, *Endgame*; for Melbourne Theatre Company: as Assistant Director: *Miss Julie.*

Jessica was Resident Director at Sydney Theatre Company from 2018–2022.

BIOGRAPHIES

JULIAN LARNACH
DRAMATURG

Julian Larnach is a Sydney-based playwright and screenwriter. He is Literary Associate at Griffin Theatre Company.

Julian's theatre credits include, as Dramaturg: for Griffin Theatre Company: *Pony*.

Other theatre credits include, as Playwright: for ATYP and Archipelago Productions: *Past the Shallows*; for Canberra Youth Theatre: *How to Vote*; for National Theatre of Parramatta: *Flight Paths*; for Darlinghurst Theatre Company: *In Real Life*; Outback Theatre for Young People: *Folk Song*; for Riverina Playwright's Commission: *Beneath an Oxbow Lake*.

Awards: Nominated: AWGIE for Best Writing, Community and Young People (*How to Vote*), AWGIE for Best Writing for Young Audiences (*Past the Shallows*); Won: Tasmanian Theatre Awards; Best Ensemble—Professional Theatre, Best New Writing, Best Production—Professional Theatre (*Past the Shallows*).

His plays have been shortlisted for Griffin Theatre Company's Lysicrates Prize, the Griffin Award for Playwriting, the Edward Albee Scholarship and the PWA Re-Gen Seed Commission. He was a member of Sydney Theatre Company's inaugural Emerging Writers Group from 2017 – 2019; an Affiliate Writer for Griffin Theatre Company; and Resident Playwright at the Australian Theatre for Young People. Julian has completed creative developments for new works with Sydney Dance Company, Playwriting Australia and Griffin Theatre Company, as well as dramaturgical secondments with Belvoir St Theatre and Melbourne Theatre Company. He has been generously supported by the Australia Council of the Arts, having undertaken a JUMP Mentorship and received an ArtStart grant.

BIOGRAPHIES

MEL PAGE
DESIGNER

As Designer: for Sydney Theatre Company: *A Raisin in the Sun*, *Lethal Indifference*; for Belvoir St Theatre: *A Taste of Honey*, *Back at the Dojo*, *Enemy of the People*, *Medea*, *Old Man*, *Small and Tired*, *The Rover*; for Melbourne Theatre Company: *A Streetcar Named Desire*, *Minnie & Liraz*; for Stuck Pigs Squealing: *Night Maybe*, *The Apocalypse Bear Trilogy*. As Set Designer: for Victorian Opera: *Noye's Fludde*. As Costume Designer: for Belvoir St Theatre: *A Christmas Carol*, *Angels in America*, *As You Like It*, *Elektra/ Oreste*, *Hamlet*, *Holding the Man*, *Ivanov*, *Jasper Jones*, *Kill the Messenger*, *Nora*, *Once in Royal David's City*, *Seventeen*, *Song of First Desire*, *Strange Interlude*, *The Glass Menagerie*, *The Government Inspector* (with Malthouse Theatre), *The Promise*; for National Theatre: *Phaedra*; for Sydney Theatre Company: *Baal* (with Malthouse Theatre), *Cat on a Hot Tin Roof*, *Les Liaisons Dangereuses*, *Mary Stuart*, *On the Beach*, *Pygmalion*, *Vs Macbeth* (with The Border Project); for Theater Basel/Residentz Theater: *Angels in America*, *Three Sisters*; for Teatr Wielki: *Medea*; for Festival Aix: *Innocence*. Bayerische Staatsoper: *Die Teufel von Loudun*, *Die Tote Stadt*, Salzburg Festival: *Greek Passion*, *Medeè*, *Lear*; for Den Norske Opera: *Pelleas et Melisande*; for Chunky Move: *The Complexity of Belonging* (with Melbourne Theatre Company and Melbourne Festival), *Depth of Field*; for Malthouse Theatre: *Pompeii L.A*; for The Hayloft Project: *Spring Awakening*, *The Only Child*, *The Suicide*; for LG Arts Center: *The Cherry Orchard*. Awards: George Fairfax Memorial Award, Sydney Theatre Award Best Costume Design, Sydney Theatre Award Best Set Design.

BIOGRAPHIES

KATE BALDWIN
LIGHTING DESIGNER

Kate Baldwin is a disabled, Japanese-Australian lighting designer. Credits as Lighting Designer include: for Sydney Theatre Company: *Top Coat*; for Belvoir St Theatre: *Lose to Win*; for Performing Lines: *Legends* (of the Golden Arches); for Darlinghurst Theatre Company & Green Door Theatre Company: *seven methods of killing kylie jenner*; for Force Majeure: *Gardener's Apprentice*; for Utp: *The Tamilization of Ahilan Ratnamohan*; for National Theatre of Parramatta: *Girl Band*, *Guards at the Taj*, *Nothing*, *Yoga Play*; for Critical Stages: *The Box Show*; for Belvoir 25A: *Forgetting Tim Minchin*, *girlfriend*; for Green Door Theatre Company: *Chewing Gum Dreams*; for New Ghosts Theatre Company: *Albion*, *Blue Christmas*; for Montague Basement: *The Great Australian Play*; for Blush Opera: *Chop Chef*.

She completed a residency at Sydney Theatre Company as Design Associate (Lighting) in 2021 and 2022. She was also a part of Ka-llective, which had residencies with PACT and Casula Powerhouse Arts Centre in 2021 and 2022.

BIOGRAPHIES

BRENDON BONEY
COMPOSER & SOUND DESIGNER

Brendon Boney is a Wiradjuri/Gamilaroi man who grew up in Wagga Wagga, New South Wales and is now based on Darkinjung country in Ettalong Beach on the Central Coast of New South Wales. Brendon's work as Sound Designer & Composer includes; for Griffin Theatre Company: *swim*; for Bangarra Dance Theatre: *Illume*, *Horizon: The Light Inside and Kulka*, *Dance Clan*; for Sydney Theatre Company: *Sweat*, *Fences*, *A Raisin in the Sun*, *The Visitors*; for Belvoir St Theatre: *Big Girls Don't Cry*, *At What Cost?*, *Lose to Win*, *Winyanboga Yurringa*; for Ensemble Theatre: *A Letter for Molly*; for National Theatre of Parramatta/Riverside Theatres: *Choir Boy*; and for Red Line Productions; *The Bugalugs Bum Thief*.

Brendon's Design Associate credits include: for Sydney Theatre Company: *The 7 Stages of Grieving and The Tempest*. His television music credits include: for ABC1: *Gods of Wheat Street*; for Network 10: *Offspring*; for Seven Network: *Winners & Losers*; and for The Nine Network: *Underbelly Chopper*. As an actor and performer, his recent credits include: for ABC: *At Home Alone Together*; for Adelaide Festival: *Stephen Page's Baleen Moondjan*; for Bangarra Dance Theatre: *Wudjang: Not the Past*; and for Illbijerri Theatre: *Black Ties*. Brendon also provided the lead character Willie's singing voice in the feature film, *Bran New Dae*.

Brendon is an established recording and performing artist and an APRA PDA winner. In the past decade, he has toured the world with the act Microwave Jenny. As a producer and songwriter Brendon's work has over 5 million streams across platforms Spotify and Apple Music.

JAMES STIBILJ
DESIGN ASSOCIATE

James is an emerging set and costume designer for stage and screen. He recently completed a Bachelor's degree in Design For Live Performance at NIDA (2021-2023).

His design credits include: for NIDA: *Sweeney Todd*, *Sandaime Richard* (winner of the APDG Emerging Designer Award). Since graduating, James has been working across theatre, opera and film as a design assistant. He has undertaken design and assistant directing secondments internationally at the Teatro dell' Opera di Roma, Toneenlhuis Antwerp and the Bayerische Staatsoper with the support of the Leslie Walford AM Award.

BIOGRAPHIES

ANDREW UNDI LEE
DEVELOPMENT ASSOCIATE

Andrew Undi Lee is a queer Korean Australian writer, director, and producer whose work spans across film, television, theatre, and webtoons. He is the recipient of the Kenneth B. Myer Award for Exceptional Talent (AFTRS) and the Young Australian Filmmaker Award from the Korean Consulate of Australia.

As Writer, his film and television credits include; for Screen Australia: *Melon Grab*; for ABC/Amazon: *Troppo*; for ABC/BBC: *Born to Spy*, *The Newsreader*; for Powerhouse Museum: *2 Moons*. He created, wrote, directed and produced the Korean Australian horror series *Night Bloomers* for SBS—which premiered at SXSW Sydney and was awarded an Australian Writers' Guild Award. He is currently writing the English-language adaptation of the Korean horror feature film *Death Bell*. As Writer's Assistant: for Netflix Australia: *Apple Cider Vinegar*; for Netflix UK: *Grown Ups*. As Director's Assistant: for Apple: *Tenzing*.

Additionally, Andrew was the Australian producer on *Saigon Kiss*, a German-Vietnamese-Australian co-produced film that was awarded the Special Mention honour by the Queer Palm Jury and currently broadcasting on ARTE TV. Andrew's theatre work includes the development of his stage play *No Asians*, written through the CAAP Artist Lab, in collaboration with Sydney Theatre Company, Belvoir St Theatre, and Griffin Theatre Company and was shortlisted for the Midsumma Queer Playwriting Award.

*This role is generously supported by **Shane** & **Cathryn Brennan**.*

BIOGRAPHIES

SHERYDAN SIMSON
PRODUCTION MANAGER

Sherydan Simson (she/they) is a Sydney-based stage and production manager passionate about creating vibrant, collaborative productions. Originally from the Coffs Harbour region, Sherydan's early experiences in community theatre sparked a lifelong love of storytelling and led them to complete a Bachelor of Fine Arts (Technical Theatre and Stage Management) at the National Institute of Dramatic Art (NIDA).

Since moving to Sydney, Sherydan has worked across a wide range of productions and events, including as Stage Manager: for Bub Productions in association with 25A: *HOT TUB*, for Hayes Theatre Co: *Pirates of Penzance (or the Slave of Duty)*, for the Sydney Conservatorium of Music: *Paper Stars*; as Production Manager: for Joshua Robson Productions in association with Hayes Theatre Co: *Little Women*, for The Other Theatre Company: *IRL*; as a Site Assistant for City of Sydney: *New Years Eve 2025* and *New Years Eve 2024*; as Access and Inclusion Assistant for City of Sydney: *Sydney Christmas Concerts 2024*.

Committed to storytelling that connects and inspires, Sherydan continues to develop a practice rooted in creativity, care, and collaboration across Australia's theatre and live events landscape.

JEN JACKSON
STAGE MANAGER

Jen Jackson is a Korean-Australian stage manager based on Gadigal land and a graduate of the National Institute of Dramatic Art, with a particular passion for new Australian work and a commitment to diversity in theatre.

As Stage Manager: for Griffin Theatre Company: *Golden Blood*, *End Of.*, *Pony*; for Contemporary Asian Australian Performance: *Double Delicious*, *The Bridal Lament*, *Lost in Shanghai*; for Belvoir St Theatre: *Lose to Win*; for Ensemble Theatre: *Master Class*; for National Theatre of Parramatta: *Nothing*. As Assistant Stage Manager: for Belvoir St Theatre: *At What Cost*, *Song of First Desire*; for Pinchgut Opera: *Rinaldo*.

BIOGRAPHIES

HEATHER JEONG
UMMA

Heather Jeong is a renowned Korean food expert, celebrated TV chef, food writer and cooking instructor. Heather's work not only showcases culinary world for media appearances and publications but also bridges the cultural heritage through storytelling and performance.

Heather's theatre credits include: for CAAP (Contemporary Asian Australian Performance): *Double Delicious* (Sydney Festival 2020, Asia TOPA and OzAsia Festival 2021).

Heather's storytelling and performance credits include: Australia Council for the Arts (Playing Australia), Longhouse CAAP (food dramaturg).

Heather's previous TV appearances include: for SBS: *Food Safari*, *The Cook Up with Adam Liaw*, *Pop Asia*, *World News*; for ABC: *Weekend*; for Channel 7: *Sunrise*; for Channel 10: *Cook's Pantry*, *My Market Kitchen*; for YTN Korea: *Documentary for Koreans living Abroad*; for KBS Korea: *Notable Koreans abroad*.

Heather's culinary presentations and performances include: The Museum of Contemporary Art; Powerhouse Museum; Melbourne Federation Square, Sydney Opera House; Good Food and Wine Show Sydney.

Heather's food writings include: SBS Kitchen Conversations; Selector; The Guardian; Taste; Coles magazine; Harris Farm magazine.

ABOUT GRIFFIN

Griffin is the only theatre company in the country exclusively devoted to the development and staging of new Australian writing. Located in the historic SBW Stables Theatre, nestled in the heart of Kings Cross, Griffin has been Australia's home for the exploration of new stories since 1979.

We are the launch pad for new plays, ideas and writing that other theatres won't take a risk on. We boldly contribute to Australia's unique and powerful storytelling culture. Plays like *Prima Facie, Holding the Man* and *City of Gold* all had their world premieres at Griffin before going out to capture the national imagination. In the words of our longest-serving Artistic Director, **Ros Horin**:

"We are the theatre of first chances."

We are passionate about nurturing emerging and established practitioners alike. We pride ourselves on supporting our vast community of artists, audiences and supporters who consider our theatre their creative home. We help ambitious, bold, risk-taking and urgent Australian work get from the page onto the stage. We tell the stories that help us know who we are as a nation, and who we want to become.

Acknowledgement of Country

Griffin Theatre Company operates and tells stories on the unceded lands of the Gadigal of the Eora Nation. We acknowledge and honour Aboriginal and Torres Strait Islander people as the oldest continuous living culture on the planet, with more than 60,000 years of storytelling practice shaping and underpinning all aspects of Australian culture. It is a privilege that we do not take lightly: to work on this land, and to tell stories on its soil.

GRIFFIN THEATRE COMPANY
13 Craigend St
Gadigal Land, Kings Cross, NSW 2011

CONTACTS
02 9332 1052
info@griffintheatre.com.au
griffintheatre.com.au

GRIFFIN FAMILY

ABOUT BELVOIR ST THEATRE

Belvoir St Theatre is a theatre company on a side street in Surry Hills, Sydney. We share our street with a park and a public housing estate, and our theatre is in an old industrial building. It has been, at various times, a garage, a sauce factory, and the Nimrod Theatre. When the theatre was threatened with redevelopment in 1984, over 600 likeminded theatre-lovers formed a syndicate to buy the building and save it from becoming an apartment block. More than thirty years later, Belvoir continues to be at the forefront of Australian acting and storytelling for the stage. At Belvoir we gather the best theatre artists we can find, emerging and established, to realise an annual season of works – new works, both Australian and international, reimagined classics and a lasting commitment to Indigenous stories. Audiences remember many landmark productions including *Counting and Cracking*, *The Drover's Wife*, *Angels in America*, *Brothers Wreck*, *The Glass Menagerie*, *Neighbourhood Watch*, *The Wild Duck*, *Medea*, *The Diary of a Madman*, *Death of a Salesman*, *The Blind Giant is Dancing*, *Hamlet*, *Cloudstreet*, *Aliwa*, *The Book of Everything*, *Keating!*, *The Exile Trilogy*, *Exit the King*, *The Sapphires*, *Faith Healer*, *FANGIRLS*, *The Jungle and the Sea* and many more. Today, under Artistic Director **Eamon Flack** and Executive Director **Aaron Beach**, Belvoir tours nationally and internationally, and continues to create its own brand of rough magic for new generations of audiences. We are proud to be creating work that speaks to life and experience in Australia and abroad, continuing our commitment to deliver diverse stories to diverse audiences. Belvoir receives government support for its activities from the federal government through the Australia Council and the state government through Create NSW. We also receive philanthropic and corporate support, which we greatly appreciate and welcome.

BELVOIR ST THEATRE
belvoir.com.au

ADDRESS
Gadigal Country
25 Belvoir St, Surry Hills, NSW 2010

CONTACTS
Box Office: +61 (2) 9699 3444
Administration: +61 (2) 9698 3344
Email: mail@belvoir.com.au

BELVOIR ST THEATRE STAFF

DIRECTORS

Artistic Director
Eamon Flack

Executive Director
Aaron Beach

ARTISTIC AND PROGRAMMING

Head of New Work
Dom Mercer

Artistic Associate
Tom Wright

Resident Director
Hannah Goodwin

Literary Associate
Ayah Tayeh

Andrew Cameron Fellow
Margaret Thanos

Balnaves Foundation Fellow
Hannah Belanszky

Balnaves Foundation Fellow
Guy Simon

PRODUCING

Head of Producing
Simone Parrott

Producer
Brittany Santargia
Emma Diaz
Emma Sampson

Artistic Administrator
Kelsey Martin

EA & ADMINISTRATION

Executive Assistant
Danielle Green

EDUCATION

Head of Education
Jane May

Education Coordinator
Nicola Denton

PRODUCTION

Head of Production
Richard Whitehouse

Production Manager
Ren Kenward

Deputy Production Manager Dana Spence

Resident Stage Manager
Luke McGettigan

Costume Supervisor
Belinda Crawford

Technical Manager
Tristan Ellis-Windsor

Senior Venue Technician
Cameron Russell

Construction Manager
Darran Whatley

Leading Hand
Jonas Trovato

Props Supervisor
Keerthi Subramanyam

MARKETING AND CUSTOMER SERVICE

Deputy Executive Director, Marketing, Community & People
Fiona Hulton

Customer Experience & Ticketing Manager
Gemma Clinch

CRM and Insights Manager
Jason Lee

Ticketing Systems Specialist & CRM Administrator
Tanya Ginori-Cairns

Box Office Coordinator
Lily Emerson

Marketing Manager
Laura Wallace

Digital Content Coordinator
Jake Severino

Communications Administrator
Kira Leiva

Front of House Manager
Alison Benstead

PUBLICITY
Kabuku PR

DEVELOPMENT

Acting Head of Development
Liz Hobart

Partnerships and Grants Coordinator
Lily O'Harte

Philanthropy Administrator
Ellen Harvey

FINANCE & OPERATIONS

Chief Financial Officer
Ash Rathod

Management Accountant
Jay Purohit

Financial Accountant
Dev Solanki

Finance Administrator
Shyleja Paul

GRIFFIN DONORS

Income from Griffin activities covers less than 40% of our operating costs—leaving an ever-increasing gap for us to fill through government funding, sponsorship and the generosity of our individual supporters. Your support helps us bridge the gap and keep ticket prices affordable and our work at its best.

To make a donation and a difference, contact Griffin on **(02) 9332 1052** or donate online at **griffintheatre.com.au**.

PROGRAM PATRONS

Griffin Ambassadors
Robertson Foundation

Griffin Amplify
Girgensohn Foundation

Griffin Literary Manager
Robertson Foundation

Griffin Redraft Fund
Shane & Cathryn Brennan

Suzie Miller Award
Suzie Miller

Griffin Studio
Gil Appleton
Darin Cooper Foundation
Kiong Lee & Richard Funston
Malcolm Robertson Foundation
Geoff & Wendy Simpson OAM

Griffin Studio Workshop
Shane & Cathryn Brennan (Patron)
Mary Ann Rolfe (Founding Patron)
Iolanda Capodanno &
Juergen Krufczyk
Darin Cooper Foundation
Bob & Chris Ernst
Jane-Maree Hurley
Susan MacKinnon
Pip Rath & Wayne Lonergan
Jake Shavikin
Merilyn Sleigh & Raoul de Ferranti

Griffin Women's Initiative
Nicole Abadee
Katrina Barter
Julieanne Campbell
Iolanda Capodanno
Jane Clifford
Jennifer Darin
Eveline Dowling
Lyndell Droga

Mandy Foley
Nicola Forrest AO
Melinda Graham
Sherry Gregory
Rosemary Hannah & Lynette
Preston
Page Henty
Jane-Maree Hurley
Tessa Leong
Susan MacKinnon
Sophie McCarthy
Suzie Miller
Sam Mostyn AC
Naomi Parry
Julia Pincus
Jo Porter
Ruth Ritchie
Lenore Robertson AM
Ann Sloan
Deanne Weir
Simone Whetton
Ali Yeldham
Anonymous (1)

PRODUCTION PARTNERS 2025

Naturism by Ang Collins
Darin Cooper Foundation
Robert Dick & Erin Shiel
Rosemary Hannah & Lynette
Preston
Kate Morgan
Bruce Meagher & Greg Waters
Julia Pincus & Ian Learmonth

SEASON DONORS

Company Patrons $100,000+
Shane & Cathryn Brennan
Neilson Foundation

Season Patrons $50,000+
Malcolm Robertson Foundation
Robertson Foundation

Mainstage Donors $20,000+
Carla Zampatti Foundation
Darin Cooper Foundation
Girgensohn Foundation
Robert Dick & Erin Shiel
Rosemary Hannah &
Lynette Preston
Julia Pincus & Ian Learmonth
Sally Breen Family Foundation
The Wales Family Foundation
Anonymous (1)

Production Donors $10,000+
Doc Ross Family Foundation
Gordon & Marie Esden
Ingrid Kaiser
Kate Morgan
Bruce Meagher & Greg Waters
Suzie Miller
Mountain Air Foundation
The Myer Foundation
The WeirAnderson Foundation

Rehearsal Donors $5,000–$9,999
Brian Abel & Mark Manton
Antoinette Albert
Gil Appleton
Melissa Ball
Lisa Barker & Don Russell
Margaret & Bernard Coles
Corinne & Bryan
Bob & Chris Ernst
Carrillo Gantner AC & Ziyin Gantner
Danny Gilbert AM & Kathleen Gilbert
Sherry Gregory
Elizabeth Hurst
The Keir Foundation
Lambert Bridge Foundation
Kiong Lee & Richard Funston
Marina Grunstein Walking Up the
Hill Foundation
Rebel Penfold-Russell OAM
Polese Foundation
Pip Rath & Wayne Lonergan
Geoff & Wendy Simpson OAM
The Skrzynski Foundation
Merilyn Sleigh & Raoul de Ferranti
Adam Suckling

Final Draft Donors $3,000–$4,999
Iolanda Capodanno & Juergen
Krufczyk
John Head
Jane-Maree Hurley
Susan MacKinnon

Workshop Donors $1,000–$2,999
Nicole Abadee & Rob Macfarlan
Emily Aitken
Baly Douglass Foundation
Katrina Barter
Cherry & Peter Best
Stephen & Annabelle Burley
Julieanne Campbell
Anna Cleary
Jane Clifford
Marijke Conrade & Robert
Henderson
Eveline Dowling
Brian Everingham

DONORS CONTINUED

Workshop Donors
$1,000–$2,999 cont.
John & Libby Fairfax
Nicholas & Rowena Falzon
Sandra & Rupert Ferman
Mandy Foley
Sandra Forbes
Hon Ben Franklin MLC
Robert Furley
Melinda Graham
Peter Graves Canberra
Mink Greene
Kate Harrison
Page Henty
David Hoskins & Paul McKnight
Susan Hyde
Colleen Kane
David & Adrienne Kitching
Benjamin Law
Tessa Leong
John Lewis
Helen Lynch AM & Helen Bauer
Patricia Lynch
Kyrsty Macdonald & Christopher Hazell
Dr Stephen McNamara
Matthew & Josephine
Sophie McCarthy
Jacqui Mercer
Catriona Morgan-Hunn
Sam Mostyn AC
Naomi Parry
Anthony Paull
Ian Phipps
Jo Porter
Kate Richardson & Chris Marrable
In memory of Katherine Robertson
Sylvia Rosenblum
Jake Shavikin
Jann Skinner
Ann & Quinn Sloan
Arahni Sont
Leslie Stern
David Sulan
Catherine Sullivan & Alexandra

Bowen
Sue Thomson
Lesley Turnbull
Janet Wahlquist
Richard Weinstein & Richard Benedict
Simone Whetton
David Williamson AO & Kristin Williamson
Elizabeth Wing
Ali Yeldham
Anonymous (6)

Reading Donors $500–$999
Jane Christensen
David Davies
Michael Diamond AM
Max Dingle OAM
Sue Donnelly
Toby Duffy
Erica Gray
Peter Gray & Helen Thwaites
James Hartwright & Kerrin D'Arcy
Michael Jackson
Greg Lamont & Gérard Wilmann
Narelle Lewis
Noella Lopez
Peter Lowry AM & Dr Carolyn Lowry OAM
Ian & Elizabeth MaCdonald
Robert Marks
Christopher Matthies & Graham Parsons
Virginia Pursell
A.O. Redmond
Steve Riethoff
Geoffrey Starr
Fiona Thomas
Mike Thompson
Samantha Turley
Julie Whitfield
Anonymous (3)

First Draft Donors $200–$499
Sally Beath
Edwina Birch
Richard Carroll

David Caulfield
Sue Clark
Edward Cooper & Daniel Zucker
Bryan Cutler
Peter & Lou Duerden
Paul & Jean Eagar
Lisa & Brad Eismen
Kevin Farmer
Robyn Fortescue & Rosie Wagstaff
Deane Golding
Sylvia Hrovatin
Matthew Huxtable
Marian & Nabeel Ibrahim
Nicki Jam
James, Beu & Sue
Ruth Lewis
George & Maruschka Loupis
Duncan McKay
Margaret Murphy
Carolyn Newman
Peter Pezzutti
Belinda Piggott & David Ojerholm
Ann Rocca
Michael & Noelleen Rosen
Kevin & Shirley Ryan
Jane S
Margaret Teh
Mary & Kerry Whitby
Rosemary White
Eve Wynhausen
Anonymous (11)

Griffin Friends Forever
We remember and honour those who have generously supported the future of Australian storytelling through a bequest to Griffin Theatre Company.

Thank you:
Annette Mary Lunney
Estate of the Late John William Roe

CURRENT AS OF 21 MAY 2025

GRIFFIN SPONSORS

Griffin would like to thank the following:

OUR PARTNERS

GOVERNMENT SUPPORTERS

Australian Government

Creative Australia

NSW GOVERNMENT

PATRON

NEILSON FOUNDATION

LEGACY BENEFACTOR

SBW Foundation

SEABORN, BROUGHTON & WALFORD FOUNDATION

CREATIVE PARTNERS

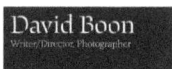

Brett Boardman Photography

David Boon
Writer/Director, Photographer

SUSU STUDIO

COPYRIGHTAGENCY CULTURAL FUND

GIRGENSOHN FOUNDATION

MALCOLM ROBERTSON FOUNDATION

PLAYKING FOUNDATION

ROBERTSON FOUNDATION

COMPANY PARTNERS

Beppi's
Established 1956

Bourke street bakery

CURRENCY PRESS

FOUR PILLARS

HOTEL INDIGO
AN IHG HOTEL
SYDNEY POTTS POINT

MARQUE

P&V WINE+LIQUOR Merchants

ROSENFELD KANT
BUSINESS ACCOUNTANTS

SYDNEY BREWERY

THE UNIVERSITY OF SYDNEY

Griffin Theatre Company is assisted by the Australian Government through Creative Australia, its principal arts investment and advisory body.
Griffin Theatre Company is supported by the NSW Government through Create NSW.

www.ingramcontent.com/pod-product-compliance
Lightning Source LLC
Chambersburg PA
CBHW050020090426
42734CB00021B/3350